CW01083584

Handbook

April 1994

British Bus Publishing

The North Midlands Bus Handbook

The North Midlands Bus Handbook is part of the Bus Handbook series that details the fleets of stage carriage and express coach operators. Where space allows other significant operators in the areas covered are also included. These Handbooks are published by British Bus Publishing and cover Scotland, Wales and England north of London. Companion volumes, The Yorkshire Bus Handbook, The Eastern Bus Handbook and The North East Bus Handbook are currently available. Handbooks for South Midlands, Wales, East Midlands, and the North West are planned for 1994. Together with the London Bus Handbooks, South East Buses and South West Buses published by Capital Transport, they provide comprehensive coverage of all the principal operators' fleets in the British Isles. Other books in the series include an annual Stagecoach Bus Handbook detailing the Stagecoach Groups operations worldwide.

Quality photographs for inclusion in these, and other areas covered by the series are welcome, though the publishers cannot accept responsibility for any loss. Details of changes to fleet information are also welcome.

More information on the Bus Handbook series is available from:

British Bus Publishing,
The Vyne,
16 St Margaret's Drive
Wellington
Telford,
Shropshire TF1 3PH

Series Editor: Bill Potter
Principal Editors for The North Midlands Bus Handbook:
Bill Potter, David Donati and Alan Mills

Acknowledgements:
We are grateful to Graham Ashworth, Keith Grimes, Martin Grosberg, Tony Hunter, Mark Jameson, Colin Lloyd, Geoff Mills, Steve Sanderson, the PSV Circle and the operating companies for their assistance in the compilation of this book.

The front cover photograph is by Bill Potter
The rear cover and frontispiece photographs are by Tony Wilson and Malc McDonald

Contents correct to March 1994

ISBN 1 897990 04 9
Published by British Bus Publishing
The Vyne, 16 St Margarets Drive, Wellington,
Telford, Shropshire, TF1 3PH
© British Bus Publishing, April 1994

Contents

ACORN TRAVEL

P J Allman, 47 Belgrave Road, Great Boughton, Chester, Cheshire, CH3 5SA

FHD741S	Bedford YLQ	Duple Dominant II	C45F	1978	Ex Ashall, Gorton, 1992
CFX308T	Ford R1114	Plaxton Supreme IV	C53F	1979	Ex Goodwin, Stockport, 1993
NIW1629	Ford R1114	Plaxton Supreme IV	C53F	1979	Ex Bradshaw, Alkrington, 1994
D39KAX	Iveco Daily 49.10	Robin Hood City Nippy	B21F	1986	Ex Rhondda, 1993
D677SEM	Renault-Dodge S56	Northern Counties	B22F	1987	Ex Rapson, Alness, 1993
D119WCC	Freight Rover Sherpa	Carlyle	B18F	1987	Ex Crosville Wales, 1992

Livery: White, turquoise and red

Previous Registrations:
NIW1629   FVC604T

Opposite upper: **K11HDC is a recent delivery to the Happy Days fleet. Seen in London, it is a Scania K113 with Van Hool Alizée body.** *Colin Lloyd*

Opposite lower: **Elcock of Madeley took delivery of this Plaxton Premiere bodied Volvo during March 1994 after a period of demonstration work for the coachbuilder. It is photographed here prior to registration, but is now registered L321JUJ.** *Plaxton Coach & Bus*

Chester bus exchange is the terminus for Acorn's Queens Road service. Previously in the Rhondda fleet D39KAX is an Iveco Daily with Robin Hood City Nippy bodywork. The livery pattern shows some evidence of the lines of its former owner. *Graham Ashworth*

ARROWEBROOK

A G Parsons, Top Farm, Croughton Road, Croughton, Cheshire, CH2 4DA

OTX59R	Bedford YMT	Caetano Estoril II	C53F	1977	Ex Gouldbourne, Royton, 1981
OFR930T	Bedford YMT	Duple Dominant II	C53F	1979	Ex Battersby-Silver Grey, 1983
HVO17V	Bedford YLQ	Duple Dominant II	C45F	1980	Ex Luxicoaches, Derby, 1985
EBB189W	Bedford YMT	Plaxton Supreme IV	C52F	1980	Ex Marsden, Sheffield, 1985
LDM441Y	Mercedes-Benz L508D	Reeve Burgess	C21F	1982	
PTX466Y	Bedford YMP	Duple Dominant IV	C35F	1982	Ex Cled Williams, Bargoed, 1986
882MMY	DAF MB200DKTL600	Plaxton Paramount 3500	C49FT	1983	Ex Cooper, Killamarsh, 1989
A787PDV	Bedford YMT	Plaxton Paramount 3200	C53F	1984	Ex Snell, Newton Abbott, 1987
B231RRU	DAF SB2305DHS585	Plaxton Paramount 3200 II	C53F	1985	Ex Priory Coaches, Gosport, 1990
D670SEM	Renault-Dodge S56	Northern Counties	B22F	1986	Ex Merseybus, 1993
D672SEM	Renault-Dodge S56	Northern Counties	B22F	1986	Ex Merseybus, 1993
D923PRJ	Freight Rover Sherpa	Made-to-Measure	M16	1987	
E463ANC	Mercedes-Benz 609D	Made-to-Measure	C24F	1988	
F368CHE	Scania K112CRB	Van Hool Alizée	C53FT	1988	Ex Elite, Stockport, 1992
G655EVN	CVE Omni	CVE	DP23F	1990	
H434DVM	Mercedes-Benz 609D	Made-to-Measure	C24F	1990	

Previous Registrations:
882MMY   VWB788Y

Livery: White and green

Arrowebrook operate one Scania K112 and this is fitted with Van Hool Alizée SH coachwork, which is the taller of the Alizée options. F368CHE is seen at the Castlefield coach park in Manchester.
Graham Ashworth

BAKERS

Guideissue Ltd, Spring Grove, Congleton Road, Biddulph, Stoke-on-Trent,
Staffordshire, ST8 7RQ

1	9530RU	Volvo B10M-60	Duple 320	C57F	1989	Ex Excelsior, Bournemouth, 1990
2	5658RU	Volvo B10M-61	Plaxton Paramount 3200 III	C49FT	1987	Ex Supreme, Coventry, 1990
3	7092RU	Volvo B10M-61	Plaxton Paramount 3200 III	C53F	1988	
4	3601RU	Volvo B10M-61	Plaxton Paramount 3200 III	C53F	1988	
5	4614RU	Volvo B10M-61	Plaxton Paramount 3200 III	C49FT	1987	Ex Excelsior, Bournemouth, 1990
6	3275RU	Volvo B10M-60	Plaxton Paramount 3200 III	C53F	1990	Ex Excelsior, Bournemouth, 1991
11	9995RU	Volvo B10M-61	Plaxton Paramount 3500 III	C49FT	1988	
12	8399RU	Volvo B10M-60	Plaxton Paramount 3500 III	C51FT	1989	
15	1879RU	Volvo B10M-60	Plaxton Paramount 3200 III	C48FT	1989	Ex Excelsior, Bournemouth, 1992
17	3353RU	Volvo B10M-60	Plaxton Paramount 3200 III	C53F	1989	Ex Excelsior, Bournemouth, 1993
19	6577RU	Mercedes-Benz 410D	Autobus Classique	M16	1992	
20	3102RU	Mercedes-Benz 811D	PMT	C21F	1989	
27	9423RU	Mercedes-Benz 811D	Optare StarRider	C29F	1989	
28	5777RU	Mercedes-Benz 609D	Whittaker Europa	C21F	1990	
29	5692RU	Mercedes-Benz 609D	Whittaker Europa	C21F	1990	
30	3093RU	Volvo B10M-60	Plaxton Paramount 3500 III	C53F	1989	Ex Parks, Hamilton, 1990
31	7025RU	Volvo B10M-60	Plaxton Paramount 3500 III	C53F	1989	Ex Parks, Hamilton, 1990
32	6280RU	Volvo B10M-60	Plaxton Paramount 3500 III	C49FT	1989	Ex Parks, Hamilton, 1991
33	3563RU	Volvo B10M-60	Plaxton Paramount 3500 III	C49FT	1989	Ex Parks, Hamilton, 1991
34	3566RU	Volvo B10M-60	Plaxton Paramount 3500 III	C38FT	1989	Ex Parks, Hamilton, 1991
35	8830RU	Mercedes-Benz 811D	Optare StarRider	C29F	1992	

Previous Registrations:

1879RU	F486LHO	3601RU	From new	7025RU	F34HGG
3093RU	F36HGG	4614RU	D255HFX	7092RU	From new
3102RU	From new	5658RU	E701HKV	8399RU	From new
3275RU	G512EFX	5691RU	From new	8830RU	From new
3353RU	F487LHO	5777RU	G428NET	9423RU	From new
3563RU	F987HGE	6280RU	F977HGE	9530RU	F477WFX
3566RU	F684EAG	6577RU	From new	9995RU	From new

Livery: Green

To accomodate the small private party, Bakers added an Mercedes-Benz 811D to the fleet in 1989 and followed it with a second in 1992. These feature the Optare StarRider body, but fitted with a single coach door as illustrated on 9423RU as it approaches Tittesworth reservoir on a summer Sunday service between Leek and Buxton. This service is operated on behalf of Staffordshire County Council.

5658RU was new to Supreme (Bonas) of Coventry in September 1987 as E701HKV. It passed to Bakers in February 1990, and carries the colours used by coaches in the Baker fleet which are not in specialist tour operators' liveries. This vehicle is a Volvo B10M-61 with a Plaxton Paramount 3200 body with the lowered driver position. *Richard Eversden*

BASSETTS

Bassetts Coachways Ltd, Transport House, Tittensor, Staffordshire, ST12 9HD

GNL712D	Bedford VAM14	Plaxton Panorama	C45F	1966	Ex Alexcars, Cirencester, 1980
RMB240	AEC Reliance 9822E	Plaxton Embassy	C41C	1967	Ex preservation, 1991
ATJ142E	Bedford VAM14	Plaxton Panorama I	C45F	1967	Ex Robinson, Great Harwood, 1973
RNR153G	Bristol LH6L	Plaxton Elite	C51F	1969	Ex Robinson, Great Harwood, 1974
NWW163K	Bristol LH6L	Plaxton Elite II	C45F	1971	Ex Robinson, Great Harwood, 1977
NWW162K	Bristol LHL6L	Plaxton Elite II	C51F	1972	Ex Robinson, Great Harwood, 1977
XTF466L	Bristol LHL6L	Plaxton Elite III	C51F	1973	Ex Robinson, Great Harwood, 1979
XTF467L	Bristol LHL6L	Plaxton Elite III	C51F	1973	Ex Robinson, Great Harwood, 1979
XTF468L	Bristol LHL6L	Plaxton Elite III	C51F	1973	Ex Robinson, Great Harwood, 1979
UTC271M	Leyland Leopard PSU5/4R	Duple Dominant	C57F	1974	Ex Robinson, Great Harwood, 1980
VTB972M	Leyland Leopard PSU5/4R	Duple Dominant	C57F	1974	Ex Robinson, Great Harwood, 1980
KCW74N	Leyland Leopard PSU5/4R	Duple Dominant	C57F	1975	Ex Robinson, Great Harwood, 1981
KCW75N	Leyland Leopard PSU5/4R	Duple Dominant	C57F	1975	Ex Robinson, Great Harwood, 1980
RFR177P	Leyland Leopard PSU3C/4R	Duple Dominant	C51F	1976	Ex Robinson, Great Harwood, 1981
JRE354V	Leyland Leopard PSU3E/4R	Plaxton Supreme IV Express	C51F	1979	Ex Middleton, Rugeley, 1981
WVH868V	Leyland Leopard PSU3E/4R	Duple Dominant II	C53F	1979	Ex Longstaff, Mirfield, 1983
LVS423V	Leyland Leopard PSU5C/4R	Duple Dominant II	C57F	1980	Ex Ebdon, Sidcup, 1983
XGS764X	Leyland Tiger TRCTL11/3R	Plaxton Supreme IV	C57F	1981	Ex Ebdon, Sidcup, 1983
XBF423X	Leyland Tiger TRCTL11/2R	Plaxton Supreme V Express	C53F	1982	
EBF806Y	Leyland Tiger TRCTL11/3R	Plaxton Paramount 3200	C57F	1983	
E93MRF	Mercedes-Benz 609D	Reeve Burgess Beaver	C25F	1988	
E542MRE	Ford Transit VE6	Dormobile	M16	1988	
E240NFA	Toyota Coaster HB31R	Caetano Optimo	C20F	1988	
F877RFP	Dennis Javelin 12SDA1907	Duple 320	C57F	1989	Ex Clarkes Coaches, Pailton, 1991
F878RFP	Dennis Javelin 12SDA1907	Duple 320	C57F	1989	Ex Clarkes Coaches, Pailton, 1992
F879RFP	Dennis Javelin 12SDA1907	Duple 320	C57F	1989	Ex Clarkes Coaches, Pailton, 1991
G472EFA	Dennis Javelin 12SDA1907	Duple 320	C57F	1990	
G278BEL	Dennis Javelin 11SDA1906	Duple 320	C57F	1989	Ex Luckett, Fareham, 1992
J4MMT	Dennis Javelin 11SDL1921	Plaxton Paramount 3200 III	C53F	1989	Ex McLaughlin, Penwortham, 1993
K440DVT	Mercedes-Benz 814D	Autobus Classique	C33F	1993	

Livery: Pale blue and grey

Bassetts of Tittensor celebrate their 45th year of operations in 1994. The 30-strong fleet of coaches includes eight Leyland Leopards mostly with Duple Dominant bodywork, with one carrying a Plaxton Supreme body. One of the Duple-bodied examples, WVH868V, is leaving Stafford for the town of Stone.
Colin Lloyd

9

BENNETTS

B A Bennett, The Garage, Kerfoot Street, Warrington, Cheshire, WA2 8HU

TNA121J	Ford R226	Plaxton Elite II	C53F	1971	Ex Flanaghan, Grappenhall, 1993
UPP437J	Ford R226	Plaxton Elite II	C53F	1971	Ex Millman, Orford, 1990
RAW35R	Bedford YLQ	Duple Dominant II	C45F	1977	Ex Tanat Valley, Pentrefelin, 1993
SFH346R	Leyland Leopard PSU3C/4R	Plaxton Supreme III	C53F	1977	Ex Barrie Hale, Warrington, 1991
JJP335V	Bedford YMT	Duple Dominant II	C53F	1980	Ex Ashton, St Helens, 1987
A291BAM	Mercedes-Benz L608D	Reeve Burgess	C21F	1984	Ex Barrie Hale, Warrington, 1991
D917VCN	Freight Rover Sherpa	Rootes	B16F	1986	Ex Northumbria, 1993
D310TWB	DAF SB2305DHS585	Van Rooijen Odyssee	C49FT	1987	Ex Barrie Hale, Warrington, 1991
E241ANB	Renault Master T35D	Advanced Vehicle Bodies	M14	1988	Ex Franklin & Bennett, Warrington, 1992

Previous Registrations:

A291BAM	A100JDF, 3672AD	TNA121J	SDL883J, LIB5964

Livery: White and blue

Sporting National Express Rapide livery is D310TWB, a rare and distinctive Van Rooijen-bodied DAF SB2300. Now in the fleet of Bennett of Warrington, it was delivered new to KM Coaches of Lundwood in South Yorkshire. The registration currently carried is its third and the vehicle is seen passing through Kingston-upon-Thames. *Colin Lloyd*

BLUE BUSES

Scragg's Coaches & Taxis, Bucknall Garage, Pennell Street, Bucknall, Stoke-on-Trent, Staffordshire, ST2 9BD

	1672VT	Bedford YMQ	Plaxton Paramount 3200	C45F	1983	Ex Evans, Tregaron, 1988
	1655VT	Mercedes-Benz 507D	Reeve Burgess	M16	1987	Ex Brown, Bathgate, 1991
63	E163TWO	Freight Rover Sherpa	Carlyle Citybus 2	B20F	1987	Ex National Welsh, 1991
69	E969SVP	Freight Rover Sherpa	Carlyle Citybus 2	B20F	1987	Ex National Welsh, 1991
96	E196UKG	Freight Rover Sherpa	Carlyle Citybus 2	B20F	1987	Ex National Welsh, 1991
97	E197UKG	Freight Rover Sherpa	Carlyle Citybus 2	B20F	1987	Ex National Welsh, 1991
	6727VT	Mercedes-Benz 507D	Made-to-Measure	C20F	1988	
78	G678XVT	Mercedes-Benz 609D	Made-to-Measure	C24F	1989	
79	G279HDW	Freight Rover Sherpa	Carlyle Citybus 2	B20F	1989	Ex National Welsh, 1992
	G675BFA	Mercedes-Benz 609D	North West CS	C24F	1990	Ex Graham's, Talke, 1993
	H304HVT	Mercedes-Benz 709D	PMT Ami	DP29F	1990	

Previous Registrations:

1655VT	E222LBV	6727VT	E416KBF, VOI3577
1672VT	DLL47Y		

Livery: Blue, or blue and white (coaches)

Scraggs of Bucknall operate minibuses in and around the Potteries using the Blue Buses fleet name. Typical of the fleet is G279HDW, a Freight Rover Sherpa with Carlyle bodywork to the Citybus 2 design. Some of the fleet carry numbers matching the last two digits of their index marks. *Keith Grimes*

BOSTOCKS

E J Bostock & Sons, Spragg Street Garage, Congleton, Cheshire, CW12 1HQ

1	J256MFP	Volvo B10M-60	Plaxton Paramount 3200 III	C57F	1992	
2	VDM937R	Bedford YLQ	Plaxton Supreme III	C45F	1977	
3	UTU550R	Bedford YLQ	Plaxton Supreme III	C45F	1977	
4	JTU228T	Bedford YLQ	Plaxton Supreme III	C45F	1979	
5	WCA942W	Leyland Leopard PSU5D/5R	Plaxton Supreme IV	C57F	1980	
6	SMB601V	Leyland Leopard PSU5D/5R	Duple Dominant II	C57F	1980	
7	OMB619P	Leyland Leopard PSU5A/4RT	Plaxton Supreme III	C57F	1976	
8	ALG130S	Leyland Leopard PSU5B/4R	Duple Dominant II	C57F	1977	
10	A817XCA	Bedford YMQ	Plaxton Paramount 3200	C45F	1984	
11	KLG106Y	Bedford YLQ	Plaxton Supreme V	C45F	1982	
12	WCA941W	Leyland Leopard PSU5D/4R	Plaxton Supreme IV	C57F	1980	
14	D437TMB	Bedford YNV Venturer	Duple 320	C53F	1987	
15	763JTU	Bedford SB1	Plaxton Consort IV	C41F	1960	
16	B847AFM	Bedford YNT	Duple Laser	C53F	1984	
17	F481KFM	Dennis Javelin 12SDA1907	Duple 320	C57F	1989	
19	UTU531R	Leyland Leopard PSU3C/4R	Plaxton Supreme III	C53F	1977	
20	JTU230T	Leyland Leopard PSU5C/4RT	Plaxton Supreme IV	C57F	1979	
22	SMB602V	Leyland Leopard PSU5D/5R	Duple Dominant II	C57F	1980	
23	E280XCA	Bedford YMP	Plaxton Paramount 3200 II	C45F	1987	
25	K456PNR	Toyota Coaster HDB30R	Caetano Optimo II	C18F	1992	
26	E281XCA	Bedford YMP	Plaxton Paramount 3200 II	C45F	1987	
27	STU260L	Leyland Leopard PSU5/4RT	Duple Dominant	C57F	1973	
29	JTU226T	Leyland Leopard PSU5C/4RT	Duple Dominant II	C57F	1979	
30	ODM193P	Leyland Leopard PSU3C/4R	Duple Dominant	C53F	1976	
31	A547RCA	Bedford YMP	Plaxton Paramount 3200	C45F	1983	
32	A560RMA	Bedford YNT	Plaxton Paramount 3200	C53F	1983	
33	A818XCA	Bedford YMQ	Plaxton Paramount 3200	C45F	1984	
35	D438TMB	Bedford YNV Venturer	Duple 320	C53F	1987	
36	BCA126W	Leyland Tiger TRCTL11/3R	Duple Goldliner IV	C57F	1981	
38	DCA552X	Bedford YMQ	Plaxton Supreme IV	C45F	1982	
39	F482KFM	Dennis Javelin 12SDA1907	Duple 320	C57F	1989	
40	DFR966W	Leyland Leopard PSU5C/4R	Duple Dominant III	C57F	1980	Ex Leyland Vehicles, 1982
41	F915KCA	Volvo B10M-61	Plaxton Paramount 3500 III	C49F	1989	
42	G956SMB	Volvo B10M-60	Plaxton Paramount 3500 III	C49F	1990	
43	LCA182X	Volvo B10M-61	Duple Goldliner IV	C49FT	1983	
44	LCA183X	Volvo B10M-61	Duple Goldliner IV	C49FT	1983	
45	H621BCA	Volvo B10M-60	Plaxton Paramount 3500 III	C49F	1991	
46	A336WCA	Leyland Tiger TRCTL11/3RH	Duple Caribbean	C49FT	1984	
47	B834CDM	Leyland Tiger TRCTL11/3R	Duple Laser	C51F	1985	
48	F447DUG	Volvo B10M-60	Plaxton Paramount 3500 III	C49FT	1989	Ex Wallace Arnold, 1993
49	F448DUG	Volvo B10M-60	Plaxton Paramount 3500 III	C49FT	1989	Ex Wallace Arnold, 1993

Livery: Fawn and red.

Photographed while operating a Cheshire Bus service is Bostocks number 30, ODM193P, one of the standard Leyland Leopards fitted with bodywork to the early Duple Dominant design. Bostocks have increased the number of stage-carriage workings in recent years and are involved in a number of town services in Congleton and 30 is seen on Buxton Old Road working a Saturday journey from Fairhouse. *Graham Ashworth*

Bostock's have always been an enthusiastic supporter of the Blackpool Coach Rally, and have won many awards for their efforts. Taking part in the competition was G956 SMB, a Volvo B10M with Plaxton Paramount 3500 bodywork. *Graham Ashworth.*

The first production Leyland Tiger to enter service is Bostock 36, BCA126W. It is seen in the Castlefield coach park in Manchester, close to the Granada studios. Another claim to fame for this vehicle is that it carries the first split-level windowed Dominant body to be built by Duple. This design employs Dominant II windows towards the front of the vehicle and the smaller, Dominant IV glass towards the rear. This is sometimes known, unofficially, as the Dominant V. *Graham Ashworth*

Until recently, Bostocks operated a number of double-deck buses, mostly on contracts. Formerly with London Buses DMS-type GHM810N, was seen here at the depot in Congleton. *Cliff Beeton*

BOULTONS OF SHROPSHIRE

MJ and CM Boulton, Sunnyside, Cardington, Church Stretton,
Shropshire, SY6 7HR

HVJ203	Bedford OB	Duple Vista	C29F	1951	Ex Mason, Mansel Lacy, 1983
KNT780	Leyland Royal Tiger PSU1/16	Burlingham Seagull	C37C	1954	Ex Vista Group, Hadnall, 1988
JBW527D	Bedford VAM3	Duple Bella Vega	C45F	1966	Ex Gain, Westfield, 1990
ODD161M	Bedford YRT	Plaxton Elite III Express	C49F	1974	Ex Harveys, Fosse Cross, 1988
JJU462N	Bedford YRQ	Plaxton Elite III	C45F	1975	Ex NCB, Wem, 1994
KUN497P	Bedford YRQ	Plaxton Elite III	C45F	1976	Ex Pearce, Yatton, 1989
SDH460R	Ford R1114	Van Hool McArdle 300	C53F	1977	Ex Boulton & Bowen, Clive, 1989
A433DUY	Bova EL28/581	Bova Europa	C53F	1984	Ex Boulton & Bowen, Clive, 1989
BXI2410	Bova FLD12.280	Bova Futura	C53F	1984	Ex Eurobus, Harmondsworth, 1987
C314NNT	Bova FLD12.250	Bova Futura	C53F	1985	Ex Boulton & Bowen, Clive, 1991
E467VNT	Mercedes-Benz 811D	Optare StarRider	DP31F	1987	
E746JAY	Dennis Javelin 11SDL1905	Plaxton Paramount 3200 III	C53F	1988	Ex Snowdon, Easington Colliery, 1992
E749NSE	Dennis Javelin 11SDL1905	Plaxton Paramount 3200 III	C53F	1988	Ex Ipswich, 1993
E536PRU	Dennis Javelin 11SDL1905	Plaxton Paramount 3200 III	C53F	1988	Ex Tillingbourne, Cranleigh, 1991
F527BUX	Mercedes-Benz 811D	Optare StarRider	DP31F	1988	
F600EAW	Ford Transit VE6	Ford	M11	1988	
G838LWR	Mercedes-Benz 811D	Optare StarRider	B31F	1990	
H84RUX	MAN 10.180	Caetano Algarve II	C35FT	1991	

Previous Registrations:
BXI2410   A118DUY

Livery: Cream, brown and orange.

Boultons is a very long-established operator based in the village of Cardington. Services are operated in the Shrewsbury, Bridgnorth and Church Stretton areas. There are three midibuses in the fleet, all Optare-bodied Mercedes-Benz 811Ds. Pictured passing through the county town of Shrewsbury is F527BUX, an example new in 1988. *Malc McDonald*

Preserved vehicles restored to full PSV standards have featured in the Boulton fleet for the past ten years. Two of these vehicles remain active; Bedford OB HVJ203 and KNT780 which is a Burlingham Seagull-bodied, first generation, Leyland Royal Tiger. This vehicle was new to Dan Gittins of Crickheath and used on his Oswestry-Liverpool and Oswestry-Manchester services between 1954 and 1959. Now it can be found on the stage services through the historic Ironbridge part of Telford.
Phillip Stephenson

There are three Plaxton-bodied Dennis Javelins in the fleet and all were acquired from other operators and carry the Paramount 3200 body design. E536PRU, shown here in Cardiff having brought the Shrewsbury Male Voice Choir to the city for the World Choir event. This vehicle came from Tillingbourne Coaches of Cranleigh in 1991.
Richard Eversden

The North Midlands Bus Handbook

BOWENS

L F Bowens Ltd, 66 Fazeley Road, Tamworth,
Staffordshire, B78 3JN

TAC235W	Volvo B58-61	Plaxton Supreme IV	C51F	1981	Ex Arnold, Tamworth, 1987
NOL44X	Volvo B58-61	Plaxton Supreme VI Express	C51F	1982	Ex Arnold, Tamworth, 1987
EEW125Y	DAF SB2300DHS585	Jonckheere Jubilee P599	C49FT	1983	Ex Arnold, Tamworth, 1987
EEW126Y	DAF SB2300DHS585	Jonckheere Jubilee P599	C49FT	1983	Ex Arnold, Tamworth, 1987
KJN299	Volvo B10M-61	Van Hool Alizée	C49FT	1983	Ex Arnold, Tamworth, 1987
A849UGB	DAF MB200DKFL600	Van Hool Alizée	C53F	1984	Ex Arnold, Tamworth, 1987
B237EOB	Bova FHD12.280	Bova Futura	C49FT	1985	Ex Arnold, Tamworth, 1987
D231POF	Bova FHD12.280	Bova Futura	C49FT	1987	Ex Arnold, Tamworth, 1987
D424POF	Bova FHD12.280	Bova Futura	C49FT	1987	Ex Arnold, Tamworth, 1987
D230PBF	Volvo B10M-61	Van Hool Alizée	C49FT	1987	Ex Arnold, Tamworth, 1987
D784SGB	Volvo B10M-61	Plaxton Paramount 3500 III	C49FT	1987	Ex Parks, Hamilton, 1988
D785SGB	Volvo B10M-61	Plaxton Paramount 3500 III	C49FT	1987	Ex Parks, Hamilton, 1988
D786SGB	Volvo B10M-61	Plaxton Paramount 3500 III	C49FT	1987	Ex Parks, Hamilton, 1988
D787SGB	Volvo B10M-61	Plaxton Paramount 3500 III	C49FT	1987	Ex Parks, Hamilton, 1988
E274HRY	Volvo B10M-61	Plaxton Paramount 3500 III	C49FT	1988	Ex Smith's, Murton, 1990
E276HRY	Bova FHD12.290	Bova Futura	C49FT	1988	Ex Black Horse Travel, London, 1990
E673JNR	Bova FHD12.290	Bova Futura	C49FT	1988	Ex Black Horse Travel, London, 1990
E599UHS	Volvo B10M-61	Plaxton Paramount 3500 III	C49FT	1988	Ex Fords Travel, Gunnislake, 1990
F30COM	Bova FHD12.290	Bova Futura	C49FT	1989	
F31COM	Bova FHD12.290	Bova Futura	C49FT	1989	
F696ONR	Bova FHD12.290	Bova Futura	C49FT	1989	Ex Moseley demonstrator, 1989
H619FUT	Bova FHD12.290	Bova Futura	C49FT	1991	
H621FUT	Bova FHD12.290	Bova Futura	C49FT	1991	
H623FUT	Bova FHD12.290	Bova Futura	C49FT	1991	
J405AWF	Bova FHD12.290	Bova Futura	C49FT	1992	
J406AWF	Bova FHD12.290	Bova Futura	C49FT	1992	
J407AWF	Bova FHD12.290	Bova Futura	C49FT	1992	
K713RNR	Toyota Coaster HDB30R	Caetano Optimo II	C18F	1992	
K714RNR	Toyota Coaster HDB30R	Caetano Optimo II	C18F	1992	
K297GDT	Bova FHD12.290	Bova Futura	C49FT	1993	
K298GDT	Bova FHD12.290	Bova Futura	C49FT	1993	
K299GDT	Bova FHD12.290	Bova Futura	C49FT	1993	
L	Scania K113CRB	Irizar Century	C49FT	1994	
L	Scania K113CRB	Irizar Century	C49FT	1994	
L	Scania K113CRB	Irizar Century	C49FT	1994	
L	Scania K113CRB	Irizar Century	C49FT	1994	

Previous Registrations:
KJN299   ODS465Y

Livery: Cream and red

The integral Bova Futura had become the standard vehicle in the Bowens fleet. Based in Tamworth, this operator's vehicles can be seen working at the NEC in Birmingham where park and ride facilities are provided for the numerous exhibitions. D424POF, one of the early examples, is seen on an excursion to Manchester. *Graham Ashworth*

K296GDT is one of Bowens newer Bova Futura's seen here in the coach park at South Mymms Services on the M25. Heading for Ostend it is working one of many excursions now undertaken to this French town. *Andy Chown*

BOYDON

DR DM RM & GM Boydon, Winkhill Filling Station, Ashbourne Road,
Winkhill, Staffordshire

AUP650L	Bedford YRQ	Plaxton Supreme III	C45F	1973	Ex Spratt, Wreningham, 1981
WWR424L	AEC Reliance 6U3ZR	Duple Dominant	C49F	1973	Ex Fisher-Ince, Market Raisen, 1982
NUS6P	AEC Reliance 6U3ZR	Plaxton Supreme III	C51F	1976	Ex Holmes, Moreton, 1989
PND719R	Bedford VAS5	Plaxton Supreme	C29F	1977	Ex Boulton & Farrimond, Wigan, 1984
SIB7882	AEC Reliance 6U3ZR	Plaxton Supreme IV	C57F	1978	Ex George, Hare Street, 1988
SIB3415	AEC Reliance 6U3ZR	Plaxton Supreme IV	C51F	1978	Ex Armstrong, Bletchley, 1988
GSU7T	AEC Reliance 6U3ZR	Plaxton Supreme III	C51F	1979	Ex Flear Coaches, Middlesbrough, 1985
XBX831T	AEC Reliance 6U3ZR	Plaxton Supreme IV	C53F	1979	Ex Eynons, Trimsaran, 1986
VVH861V	Ford Transit 190	Reeve Burgess	C17F	1979	Ex Moorland Rover, Werrington, 1991
SIB3053	AEC Reliance 6U3ZR	Plaxton Supreme IV	C53F	1980	Ex Holden, Dudley, 1993
4195PX	Leyland Tiger TRCTL11/3R	Plaxton Paramount 3500	C49FT	1982	Ex Caddishead Coaches, 1993
TIB2865	Leyland Tiger TRCTL11/3R	Plaxton Paramount 3200	C57F	1982	Ex Walls, Wigan, 1993
MIB4964	Leyland Tiger TRCTL11/3R	Plaxton Paramount 3500	C50F	1983	Ex Bordian, Darwen, 1989
A891EBC	Mercedes-Benz L307D	Reeve Burgess	M12	1983	Ex Heritage Tours, Hyde, 1994
NIW5986	Mercedes-Benz L608D	Reeve Burgess	C21F	1984	Ex Flintham, Metheringham, 1993
RIB8034	Mercedes-Benz L608D	Mellor	C21F	1985	Ex Booth, Bury, 1992

Previous Registrations:

4195PX	WBV940Y	RIB8034	C612ADB	SIB7882	EBM446T
MIB4964	THY293Y	SIB3053	PRO445Y	TIB2865	CLD886Y
NIW5986	A132MFL	SIB3415	EBM457T		

Livery: White, red, yellow and orange.

Boydon's were running services from Leek to the villages of Winkhill and Cauldon Lowe well before deregulation, and have run continuously since then. A keen enthusiast for the AEC product, the Boydon fleet contains many examples of the Reliance, all bar one with Plaxton bodywork. SIB 3053 is a recent example fitted with the Supreme III body design. *Graham Ashworth.*

BRITANNIA

Wrekin Coach Services Ltd, Travel House, 17 Market Street, Oakengates, Telford, Shropshire, TF2 6EL

Depots: Coach Garage, Donnington Wood, Telford.

1	NIW6131	DAF MB230DKFL615	Van Hool Alizée	C55F	1988	Ex Robinsons, Great Harwood, 1992
2	NIW2322	DAF MB230DKFL615	Van Hool Alizée	C55F	1988	Ex Robinsons, Great Harwood, 1992
3	GIL3273	DAF MB200DKFL600	Plaxton Paramount 3500 II	C49F	1985	Ex Happy Days, Woodseaves, 1987
4	GIL3274	DAF SB2300DHS585	Plaxton Paramount 3200	C55F	1984	Ex Meadway, Birmingham, 1988
5	GIL3275	Leyland Tiger TRCTL11/3RH	Plaxton Supreme V	C53F	1984	Ex Robinsons, Great Harwood, 1989
7	OIW5807	DAF MB230DKFL615	Plaxton Paramount 3500 III	C53F	1988	Ex , 1994
6	NIW3546	Volvo B10M-60	Plaxton Paramount 3500 III	C53F	1989	Ex Parks, Hamilton, 1991
8	GNT433V	Ford R1114	Plaxton Supreme IV	C53F	1980	
9	GIL1909	Leyland Tiger TRCTL11/3R	Plaxton Paramount 3200	C57F	1984	Ex Stevensons, 1991
11	GNT434V	Ford R1114	Plaxton Supreme IV	C53F	1980	
14	GNT432V	Ford R1114	Plaxton Supreme IV	C53F	1980	
15	OIW7115	DAF MB230DKFL615	Van Hool Alizée	C55F	1987	Ex Fishwick, Leyland, 1994
17	NIW2317	DAF SB2305DHS585	Duple 320	C57F	1988	
18	NIW2318	DAF MB230DKFL615	Plaxton Paramount 3500 III	C53F	1987	
20	NIW2320	DAF MB230DKFL615	Van Hool Alizée	C55F	1987	Ex Fishwick, Leyland, 1994
21	NIW2321	Leyland Tiger TRCTL11/3RZ	Plaxton Paramount 3200 III	C57F	1987	Ex Priory Coaches, Gosport, 1990
22	KAD349V	Leyland Leopard PSU5C/4R	Plaxton Supreme IV	C57F	1979	Ex Cook, Biggleswade, 1986
23	OIW7023	DAF SB2300DHS585	Plaxton Paramount 3200	C55F	1984	Ex Wombwell Coaches, 1994
24	BGK314S	Leyland Leopard PSU5C/4R	Plaxton Supreme III	C55F	1978	Ex Epsom Coaches, 1987
25	GIL2195	Leyland Tiger TRCTL11/3R	Plaxton Paramount 3200	C57F	1983	Ex Warren, Tenterden, 1991
26	OIW7026	Leyland Tiger TRCTL11/3R	Plaxton Supreme V	C53F	1982	Ex Robinsons, Great Harwood, 1989
27	OIW7027	Leyland Tiger TRCTL11/3R	Plaxton Supreme V	C53F	1982	Ex Robinsons, Great Harwood, 1989
28	J129VAW	Mercedes-Benz 814D	Reeve Burgess Beaver		1991	
29	H177EJF	Toyota Coaster HDB30R	Caetano Optimo	C21F	1991	
30	GHE739V	Leyland Leopard PSU5C/4R	Plaxton Supreme IV	C57F	1980	Ex Mountford, Manchester, 1990

Previous Registrations:

GHE739V	YHG189V, 170BHR	NIW2317	E832YAW	NIW6131	D218YCW
GIL1909	A834PPP	NIW2318	E176VUJ	OIW5807	E602LSL
GIL2195	XCD138Y	NIW2320	D277XCX	OIW7023	A828GFP
GIL3273	B879AJX	NIW2321	D103ERU	OIW7026	LEC196X
GIL3274	B996BOJ	NIW2322	D214YHG	OIW7027	LEC197X
GIL3275	A204OCW	NIW3546	F976HGE	OIW7115	D275XCX

Livery: Blue and yellow

For a short period after de-regulation, Britannia operated commercial stage services in the new town of Telford, but most of the service now consists of tendered operation and contracts. Ford R1114 GNT433V has a Plaxton Supreme IV body and is seen heading for Wellington. *Bill Potter*

A contrast in chassis is demonstrated in this photograph of two Plaxton Paramount 3200s. On the left is Leyland Tiger GIL3275, while to the right is the same body style based on a DAF SB2300. The vehicles were photographed at the depot in Donnington Wood, part of north Telford. *Bill Potter*

BURTON BUS COMPANY

Andre Al-Hamid, Stee Fabs Industrial Estate, Victoria Crescent, Burton-on-Trent, Staffordshire, DE14 2QD

JVK223P	Bedford VAS5	Duple Dominant	C29F	1976	Ex Heath, Barwell, 1993
NBF743P	Ford R1114	Duple Dominant	C53F	1976	Ex Zamir, Burton, 1993
PKX274R	Ford R1114	Plaxton Supreme III	C53F	1977	Ex Barratt, Nantwich, 1993
AUE368S	Bedford VAS5	Plaxton Supreme III	C29F	1978	Ex Evans, Tregaron, 1993
WDB552S	Ford R1114	Duple Dominant II	C53F	1978	Ex Barratt, Nantwich, 1993
MBT676T	Ford R1114	Plaxton Supreme III	C53F	1978	Ex Omfield, Shepshed, 1993
DNK440T	Ford Transit 190	Dormobile	M16	1979	Ex Zamir, Burton, 1993
YHB21T	Leyland Leopard PSU5C/4R	Duple Dominant II	C53F	1979	Ex Vanguard, Bedworth, 1993
XRF368X	Ford Transit 190	Dormobile	M16L	1982	Ex Zamir, Burton, 1993
CBA215Y	Ford Transit 190	Mellor	M16	1983	Ex Zamir, Burton, 1993
D820PUK	Freight Rover Sherpa	Carlyle	B18F	1987	Ex Zamir, Burton, 1993
F966LTY	Mercedes-Benz 407D	Reeve Burgess	M15	1989	Ex Zamir, Burton, 1993
F473ABO	Mercedes-Benz 408D	Devon Conversions	M15	1989	Ex Easyway, Pencoed, 1993

Previous Registrations:
AUE368S   RTS629S, 390FAU

BUTTERS

S Butter & Partners, Yew Tree Cottage, Village Road, Childs Ercall, Shropshire, TF9 2DG

OOU534M	Bedford YRT	Plaxton Elite III	C53F	1973	Ex Epsom Coaches, 1979
TMJ633R	Bedford YMT	Duple Dominant II	C53F	1977	Ex Turner, Brown Edge, 1984
UWJ628S	Bedford YMT	Plaxton Supreme III	C53F	1978	Ex Shaw, Barnsley, 1981
UUX842S	Bedford YMT	Plaxton Supreme III Express	C53F	1978	Ex Williamsons, Shrewsbury, 1988
YUJ416T	Bedford YMT	Duple Dominant II	C53F	1978	
VWX352X	Bova EL26/581	Bova Europa	C51F	1982	Ex Kingswood Coaches, 1989
TFG221X	Leyland Leopard PSU5E/4R	Plaxton Supreme V	C50F	1982	Ex Brighton & Hove, 1989
HIL8863	DAF MB200DKFL600	LAG Galaxy	C53F	1983	
AUT842Y	Mercedes-Benz L307D	Reeve Burgess	M12	1983	Ex Boulton, Cardington, 1986
DXI1454	Leyland Royal Tiger RTC	Leyland Doyen	C50F	1984	Ex Bennett, Warrington, 1992

Previous Registrations:
DXI1454   A483MHG   HIL8863   PBX280Y

Livery: White and blue

Newport, Shropshire, is a market town now dominated by near-by Telford. However, its location attracts many different operators onto the various Shropshire Bus contracts which serve the town. Passing through, while performing school duties is Butters VWX352X, a Bova Europa. *Bill Potter*

Butters are based in the village of Childs Ercall in north Shropshire. They provide rural services for schools, together with market day services for several villages to the popular towns such as Market Drayton and Wellington. The newest vehicle in the Butters fleet is a Leyland Royal Tiger, DXI1454, seen while on an excursion. *Graham Ashworth*

CHASE BUS SERVICES

Chase Coaches Ltd, No Name Road, Chasetown, Walsall, Staffordshire, WS7 8FS

1	THX117S	Leyland National 10351A/2R	B36D	1978	Ex London Buses, 1992
2	OJD858R	Leyland National 10351A/2R	B36D	1977	Ex London Buses, 1992
3	AYR309T	Leyland National 10351A/2R	B35D	1979	Ex Eastbourne, 1990
4	YYE274T	Leyland National 10351A/2R	B35D	1979	Ex Eastbourne, 1990
5	AYR339T	Leyland National 10351A/2R	B35D	1979	Ex Eastbourne, 1990
6	YYE295T	Leyland National 10351A/2R	B35D	1979	Ex Eastbourne, 1990
7	THX151S	Leyland National 10351A/2R	B36F	1978	Ex London Buses, 1990
8	THX181S	Leyland National 10351A/2R(Leyland 0680)	B36F	1978	Ex London Buses, 1990
9	BYW365V	Leyland National 10351A/2R	B36F	1979	Ex London Buses, 1990
10	MRP5V	Leyland National 10351A/2R(Leyland 0680)	B43F	1979	Ex London Buses, 1990
11	THX260S	Leyland National 10351A/2R	B36F	1978	Ex London Buses, 1990
12	OJD863R	Leyland National 10351A/2R	B36F	1977	Ex London Buses, 1990
14	MMB970P	Leyland National 11351/1R/SC	DP48F	1976	Ex Crosville Wales, 1990
15	THX222S	Leyland National 10351A/2R	B36D	1978	Ex London Buses, 1990
16	THX236S	Leyland National 10351A/2R	B36D	1978	Ex London Buses, 1990
17	GHU639N	Leyland National 10351/1R	B41F	1975	Ex Country Bus, Atherington, 1990
18	HHU632N	Leyland National 10351/1R	B44F	1975	Ex County, Leicester, 1989
19	NEN957R	Leyland National 11351A/1R	B49F	1977	Ex County, Leicester, 1989
20	KBC110N	Leyland National 10351/1R	B41F	1975	Ex County, Leicester, 1989
21	NEN965R	Leyland National 11351A/1R	B49F	1977	Ex County, Leicester, 1989
22	NWO467R	Leyland National 11351/1R	DP48F	1977	Ex Burrows, Ogmore Vale, 1993
23	HUH409N	Leyland National 10351/1R	B41F	1975	Ex Amberley, Pudsey, 1989

Chase Bus Services has achieved considerable growth in its fleet since de-regulation and has now reached a strength of almost 80 units. The bus fleet is mostly composed of Leyland Nationals of a wide range in terms of age, model, and length. Services have been developed in Walsall and the surrounding Black Country and Staffordshire Chase areas. BYW418V is one of many units in the fleet to have originated with London Transport. It was re-engined with a Leyland 0680 engine, and the result of this modification is demonstrated by the rear nearside grill. It has recently been re-registered MRP5V. *Tim Weatherup*

24	WBN464T	Leyland National 11351A/1R		B49F	1979	Ex Tanat Valley, Pentrefelin, 1993
25	LTG796P	Leyland Leopard PSU3C/2R	East Lancashire	B51F	1976	Ex Inter Valley Link, 1989
26	LTG797P	Leyland Leopard PSU3C/2R	East Lancashire	B51F	1976	Ex Inter Valley Link, 1989
27	LTG798P	Leyland Leopard PSU3C/2R	East Lancashire	B51F	1976	Ex Inter Valley Link, 1989
28	LTG850P	Leyland Leopard PSU4C/2R	East Lancashire	B45F	1976	Ex Inter Valley Link, 1989
29	PPM894R	Leyland National 11351A/1R		B49F	1977	Ex Clyde Coast, Ardrossen, 1993
30	RKA870T	Leyland National 11351A/1R		B52F	1979	Ex Merseybus, 1991
31	THX160S	Leyland National 10351A/2R		B36D	1978	Ex London Buses, 1992
32	NFM856M	Leyland National 1151/1R/0405		DP48F	1974	Ex Crosville Wales, 1988
33	ORP465M	Leyland National 1151/1R/0401		B49F	1974	Ex United Counties, 1988
34	KNW656N	Leyland National 11351/1R		B52F	1975	Ex West Yorkshire, 1988
35	HCA970N	Leyland National 11351/1R/SC		B48F	1975	Ex Crosville Wales, 1988
36	HCA969N	Leyland National 11351/1R/SC		DP48F	1974	Ex Crosville Wales, 1987
37	GMA403N	Leyland National 11351/1R/SC		DP48F	1974	Ex Crosville Wales, 1987
38	HMA658N	Leyland National 11351/1R/SC		DP48F	1974	Ex Crosville Wales, 1987
39	HFM183N	Leyland National 11351/1R/SC		B48F	1974	Ex Crosville Wales, 1987
40	THX209S	Leyland National 10351A/2R		B36D	1978	Ex London Buses, 1990
41	EGB78T	Leyland National 11351A/1R		B52F	1979	Ex Western Scottish, 1991
42	THX193S	Leyland National 10351A/2R		B36D	1978	Ex London Buses, 1990
43	OJD868R	Leyland National 10351A/2R		B35D	1977	Ex Eastbourne, 1991
44	OJD870R	Leyland National 10351A/2R		B36D	1977	Ex Black Prince, Morley, 1990
45	EGB94T	Leyland National 11351A/1R		B52F	1979	Ex Western Scottish, 1991
46	OJD865R	Leyland National 10351A/2R		B36D	1977	Ex London Buses, 1992
47	RTE111G	Leyland Leopard PSU3A/2R	East Lancashire	B51F	1969	Ex Lancaster, 1983
48	HNE651N	Leyland National 10351/1R		B41F	1975	Ex Greater Manchester, 1987
49	HJA127N	Leyland National 10351/1R		B41F	1975	Ex Greater Manchester, 1987
50	THX149S	Leyland National 10351A/2R		B44F	1978	Ex Parfitts, Rhymney Bridge, 1993
51	THX159S	Leyland National 10351A/2R		B44F	1978	Ex Parfitts, Rhymney Bridge, 1993
52	THX266S	Leyland National 10351A/2R		B44F	1978	Ex Parfitts, Rhymney Bridge, 1993
53	THX264S	Leyland National 10351A/2R		B44F	1978	Ex Parfitts, Rhymney Bridge, 1993
54	YYE270T	Leyland National 10351A/2R		B36D	1979	Ex Parfitts, Rhymney Bridge, 1993
55	AYR317T	Leyland National 10351A/2R		B44F	1979	Ex Parfitts, Rhymney Bridge, 1993
56	AYR330T	Leyland National 10351A/2R		B44F	1979	Ex Parfitts, Rhymney Bridge, 1993
57	AYR343T	Leyland National 10351A/2R		B44F	1979	Ex Parfitts, Rhymney Bridge, 1993
58	YPF773T	Leyland National 10351A/1R		B41F	1979	Ex Sovereign Bus & Coach, 1993

In addition to the Leyland Nationals, Chase operate four Leyland Leopards from the Inter Valley Link operation taken over by National Welsh in 1989. These vehicles all have East Lancashire bodywork as shown by LTG850P, passing through Lichfield.
Graham Ashworth

250	E834EVS	Ford Transit VE6	Chassis Developments	M16	1988	
251	PSU988	Volvo B10M-61	Caetano Algarve	C53F	1986	Ex Parks, Hamilton, 1990
252	PSU989	Volvo B10M-61	Caetano Algarve	C53F	1986	Ex Parks, Hamilton, 1990
253	PSU987	Volvo B10M-61	Caetano Algarve	C53F	1985	Ex OK, Bishop Auckland, 1989
254	FSV428	Volvo B10M-60	Plaxton Paramount 3500 III	C49F	1983	Ex Harry Shaw, Coventry, 1992
255	PSU954	Leyland Tiger TRCTL11/3R	Plaxton Viewmaster IV	C50F	1983	Ex Hurlock, Northfleet, 1988
256	PSU942	Volvo B10M-61	Van Hool Alizée	C49FT	1988	Ex Excelsior, Bournemouth, 1993
257	PSU969	Volvo B10M-61	Van Hool Alizée	C49FT	1984	Ex Shearings, 1991
258	PSU906	Volvo B10M-61	Duple Caribbean	C46FT	1983	Ex S U T, 1991
259	YBJ403	DAF MB230DKFL615	Jonckheere Jubilee P50	C51F	1988	Ex Hallmark, Luton, 1992
260	PSU946	Volvo B10M-61	Plaxton Paramount 3500 III	C49FT	1988	Ex Limebourne, Battersea, 1993
261	A105YOX	Bedford YNT	Plaxton Paramount 3200	C53F	1984	
262	E860WYC	Ford Transit VE6	Dormobile	M16	1988	Ex Farthing Corner, 1993
263	G880ELJ	Ford Transit VE6	Zodiac	M14	1990	Ex Conveyor Services Europe, 1993

Previous Registrations:

A105YOX	A358KFD, PSU946	PSU954	KGS488Y
FSV428	F32VAC, COV8V, EJI3935	PSU969	A197MNE
KBC110N	JNB998N, 531PP	PSU987	B801MDC
MRP5V	BYW418V	PSU988	C678KDS
PSU906	THL298Y	PSU989	C682KDS
PSU942	XEL254, E749SEL	YBJ403	E682NNH
PSU946	E302OMG		

Livery: Orange, brown and white; Coaches - white, red and blue or Silver blue metallic.

Chase also has a coach fleet, the livery for which is in total contrast to the buses, featuring a metallic mid-blue. The coaches are now numbered in a series starting from 200. PSU946, shown here as 61, but now carrying 261, is the only Bedford in the fleet. It is a Plaxton-bodied YNT which was new to Chase before de-regulation. It has recently swapped its private number with a Volvo acquired in 1993.
Richard Eversden

CHESTER

Chester City Transport Ltd, Station Road, Chester, Cheshire, CH1 3AD

1	B201EFM	Leyland Olympian ONLXB/1R	Northern Counties	DPH43/30F	1985	
2	B202EFM	Leyland Olympian ONLXB/1R	Northern Counties	DPH43/30F	1985	
3	B203EFM	Leyland Olympian ONLXB/1R	Northern Counties	DPH43/32F	1985	
4	B204EFM	Leyland Olympian ONLXB/1R	Northern Counties	DPH43/32F	1985	
5	VRA124Y	Leyland Olympian ONLXB/1R	Northern Counties	H43/28F	1982	Ex Derby, 1987
6	VRA125Y	Leyland Olympian ONLXB/1R	Northern Counties	H43/28F	1982	Ex Derby, 1987
7	UWW1X	Leyland Olympian ONLXB/1R	Roe	H47/29F	1982	Ex West Yorkshire PTE, 1987
8	UWW2X	Leyland Olympian ONLXB/1R	Roe	H47/29F	1982	Ex West Yorkshire PTE, 1987
9	F209JMB	Leyland Olympian ONCL10/2RZ	Northern Counties	DPH45/32F	1989	
10	F210JMB	Leyland Olympian ONCL10/2RZ	Northern Counties	DPH45/33F	1989	
11	F882VSJ	Leyland Olympian ONCL10/1RZ	Leyland	H47/31F	1988	Ex A1 (McKinnon), Ardrossan, 1991
12	A976OST	Leyland Olympian ONLXB/1R	Alexander RL	H45/30F	1984	Ex Highland Scottish, 1991
13	C378CAS	Leyland Olympian ONLXB/1RH	Alexander RL	H45/32F	1986	Ex Highland Scottish, 1991
14	C379CAS	Leyland Olympian ONLXB/1RH	Alexander RL	H45/32F	1986	Ex Highland Scottish, 1991
15	C380CAS	Leyland Olympian ONLXB/1RH	Alexander RL	H45/32F	1986	Ex Highland Scottish, 1991
24	A157MCK	Leyland Tiger TRCTL11/3R	Duple Dominant IV	C55F	1983	Ex Kirkham, Oswaldtwistle, 1988
25	E25BTU	Dennis Javelin 11SDL1905	Duple 320	C55F	1988	
26	A66KVM	Leyland Tiger TRCTL11/3R	Plaxton Paramount 3200	C55F	1984	Ex GM Buses, 1990
27	A67KVM	Leyland Tiger TRCTL11/3R	Plaxton Paramount 3200	C55F	1984	Ex GM Buses, 1990
28	XFM211	Leyland Tiger TRCTL11/3R	Plaxton Paramount 3200	C55F	1984	Ex GM Buses, 1989
29	E43SBO	Dennis Javelin 11SDA1906	Duple 320	C51F	1988	Ex Bebb, Llantwit Fardre, 1989
30	E126LAD	Hestair Duple 425 SDA1512	Duple	C53FT	1988	Ex Swanbrook, Cheltenham, 1993

Chester 5 (VRA124Y) is one of a pair of Northern Counties-bodied Leyland Olympians formerly in the Derby fleet, being replaced when that operator decided to standardise on Volvo Citybuses in 1987. It is pictured about to leave Chester for Saltney Ferry. *Mike Fowler*

34-41

		Renault-Dodge S56			Northern Counties		B22F*	1987-88	*39-41 are DP23F		
34	E134XCA	36	E136XCA	38	E38YFM	40	E40YMB	41	E41YMB
35	E135XCA	37	E137XCA	39	E39YMB				

42-48

		Renault-Dodge S56			Alexander AM		B23F	1987-88	Ex Grimsby-Cleethorpes, 1989		
42	D36NFU	44	D38NFU	46	E40PJV	47	E41PJV	48	E42PJV
43	D37NFU	45	D39NFU				

51-60

		Dennis Dart 9SDL3011			Plaxton Pointer		B35F	1991-93			
51	J51EDM	53	J53EDM	55	J155EDM	57	K57LLG	59	K59LLG
52	J52EDM	54	J54EDM	56	K56LLG	58	K58LLG	60	L160PDM

61	L61PDM	Dennis Dart 9SDL3021	Plaxton Pointer	B35F	1993
62	L62PDM	Dennis Dart 9SDL3021	Plaxton Pointer	B35F	1993
63	L63SFM	Dennis Dart 9SDL3031	Plaxton Pointer	B35F	1994
64	L64SFM	Dennis Dart 9SDL3031	Plaxton Pointer	B35F	1994
75	OFM957K	Daimler Fleetline CRG6LX(6LXB)	Northern Counties (1985)	H43/29F	1972	
77	TWH694T	Leyland Fleetline FE30AGR	Northern Counties	H43/32F	1978	Ex GM Buses, 1990
78	HDB124V	Leyland Fleetline FE30AGR	Northern Counties	H43/32F	1980	Ex GM Buses, 1990
79	BCB613V	Leyland Fleetline FE30AGR	Northern Counties	H43/32F	1980	Ex GM Buses, 1990
80	DWH682W	Leyland Fleetline FE30AGR	Northern Counties	H43/32F	1980	Ex GM Buses, 1990

87-98

		Leyland Fleetline FE30AGR			Northern Counties		H43/29F*	1978-80	*87/92/5-8 are O43/16F		
87	CFM87S	92	KFM192T	94	SDM94V	96	SDM96V	98	SDM98V
90	KFM190T	93	KFM193T	95	SDM95V	97	SDM97V		

Opposite top: **The Reeve Burgess-designed Beaver on the Dennis Dart has continued to be produced by Plaxton, now a member of the Henleys group. Chester 53, J53EDM, is one of a batch of five similar vehicles which entered service in 1991 with similar deliveries following in 1993 and 1994. The vehicle is awaiting departure from Chester bus exchange for the village of Christleton.** *Richard Eversden*

Opposite bottom: **There are seven coaches in the Chester fleet, two of which are Dennis Javelins. The origin of this vehicle 29, E43SBO, fitted with a Duple 320 body, is given away in the registration. It was new to Bebb of Llantwit Fardre in South Wales and came to Chester in 1989.** *Richard Eversden*

Increasing numbers of Britain's heritage towns and cities have developed tourist sightseeing services. Many of these tours are operated by open top double deckers. In recent years, perhaps surprisingly, these services seem to have attracted competition. This has happened in Chester, where Guide Friday has operated in opposition to the established operator. Thus, perhaps, Chester 95, SDM95V, a Northern Counties-bodied Leyland Fleetline sports the legend 'The Original Chester Tour' rather in the style of London Buses.
Mike Fowler

99-103

Dennis Dominator DD121B Northern Counties H43/29F 1981

99	YMA99W	100	YMA100W	101	YMA101W	102	YMA102W	103	YMA103W

104-112

Dennis Dominator DDA150* Northern Counties H43/29F 1982-83 *110-112 are DDA170

104	HMA104X	106	HMA106X	108	KLG108Y	110	A110UCA	112	A112UCA
105	HMA105X	107	KLG107Y	109	KLG109Y	111	A111UCA		

119	LFV101X	Dennis Dominator DD138	East Lancashire	H45/33F	1981	Ex Hyndburn, 1988
120	LFV102X	Dennis Dominator DD138	East Lancashire	H45/33F	1981	Ex Hyndburn, 1988
121	OCS34X	Dennis Dominator DDA151	East Lancashire	H45/31F	1981	Ex A1 (Duff), Ardrossan, 1988
126	DBV3W	Dennis Dominator DD120	East Lancashire	H43/31F	1981	Ex Warrington, 1989
127	DBV4W	Dennis Dominator DD120	East Lancashire	H43/31F	1981	Ex Warrington, 1990
129	SCW103X	Dennis Dominator DDA158	East Lancashire	H43/33F	1982	Ex Hyndburn, 1990
130	SCW104X	Dennis Dominator DDA158	East Lancashire	H43/33F	1982	Ex Hyndburn, 1990
131	A105KRN	Dennis Dominator DDA158	East Lancashire	H43/33F	1983	Ex Hyndburn, 1990
132	A106KRN	Dennis Dominator DDA158	East Lancashire	H43/33F	1983	Ex Hyndburn, 1990
133	B107UFV	Dennis Dominator DDA950	East Lancashire	H43/33F	1985	Ex Hyndburn, 1990
134	B108UFV	Dennis Dominator DDA950	East Lancashire	H43/33F	1985	Ex Hyndburn, 1990
135	JSL282X	Dennis Dominator DD139	East Lancashire	H50/33F	1981	Ex Brighton, 1991
136	JSL283X	Dennis Dominator DD139	East Lancashire	H50/33F	1981	Ex Brighton, 1991
137	JSL284X	Dennis Dominator DD139	East Lancashire	H50/33F	1981	Ex Brighton, 1991
140	MPN140W	Dennis Dominator DD122	East Lancashire	H47/35F	1980	Ex Eastbourne, 1992
141	MPN141W	Dennis Dominator DD122	East Lancashire	H47/35F	1980	Ex Eastbourne, 1992

Previous Registrations:

SND83X HNE643N XFM211 A54KVM

Livery: Cream and maroon.
White, red and blue (Park & Ride): 1, 2, 133 and 134.
The Original Chester Tour: 87, 92/5/7.
The Liverpool Tour: 96, 98

Chester City Transport provide Park & Ride facilities in the city using four double-deck buses in a livery of white, blue and red. Two Dennis Dominators and two Leyland Olympians are employed and one of the latter, 2 B202EFM, is seen at the bus exchange working service 31.
Graham Ashworth

CLOWES

GA & KM Clowes, Barrow Moor Farm, Barrow Moor, Longnor,
Staffordshire, SK17 0QP

MRH162P	Bedford YRQ	Duple Dominant	C45F	1976	Ex Leech, Macclesfield, 1988
RAW32R	Bedford YMT	Duple Dominant	C53F	1977	Ex Bryant's Coaches, Williton, 1989
CYH578V	Ford Transit 160	Clowes	M12	1979	
GJF576V	Bedford YMT	Van Hool Aragon	C53F	1979	Ex Bailliss, Barton, 1987
VRY1X	DAF MB200DKTL600	Smit Euro Hi-Liner	C53F	1982	Ex Robin Hood, Rushton, 1990
C386VBC	Bedford YNV Venturer	Willowbrook Crusader	C51FT	1986	Ex Alpha Coaches, Coventry, 1992
D770JUB	Freight Rover Sherpa	Dormobile	B20F	1987	Ex Yorkshire Rider, 1991
D710SKU	Freight Rover Sherpa	Crystals	M16	1986	Ex Non psv, 1988
RIB3524	Aüwaerter Neoplan N216H	Aüwaerter Jetliner	C53F	1986	Ex Robin Hood, Rudyard, 1993

Previous Registrations:
RIB3524   C718JTL

Livery: Orange and green.

C386VBC is an uncommon type of vehicle, a Willowbrook Crusader-bodied Bedford Venturer, photographed at High Peak College in Buxton. This vehicle was acquired in a derelict state and has been fully refurbished by Clowes. *Graham Ashworth*

CLUN VALLEY

WM & JM Price, Coach Garage, Newcastle, Shrewsbury
Shropshire, SY7 8QL

HLG812K	Bedford VAL70	Plaxton Elite II	C53F	1972	Ex Lakelin, Felindre, 1989
WNL382A	Volvo B58-56	Caetano Alpha	C53F	1978	Ex Filer, Ilfracombe, 1991
LTH742	Volvo B58-56	Plaxton Supreme IV	C42FT	1980	Ex Evans, Tregaron, 1991
PNM694W	Bedford YMQ	Duple Dominant II	C35F	1980	Ex Berwyn Coaches, Trefor, 1992
ORY708W	Bedford YMT	Duple Dominant II	C53F	1981	Ex Reliant, Ibstock, 1993
JTC993X	Renault-Dodge S66	Reeve Burgess	B21F	1982	Ex Evans, Tregaron, 1993
A512LPP	Bedford YMQ	Plaxton Paramount 3200	C35F	1983	Ex Miller, Box, 1993
D945OKK	Peugeot-Talbot Express	Talbot	M14	1987	Ex Bennett, Bournemouth, 1991
E98LBC	Dennis Javelin 11SDA1906	Duple 320	C53F	1988	Ex Evans, Tregaron, 1993
G27RVJ	Freight Rover Sherpa	Freight Rover	M16	1989	

Previous Registrations:

LTH742	KHL559W	WNL382A	AWB319T

Livery: Black, beige and gold.

Copeland's Tours operate MIB279, one of three Leyland Tigers obtained from the Wessex fleet in 1991. This view of the near side, taken at the depot in Meir, demonstrates the express door variant of the Paramount 3200 model. *Graham Ashworth*

COPELAND

Copeland Tours (Stoke on Trent) Ltd, Uttoxeter Road, Meir, Stoke-on-Trent, Staffordshire

MIB520	Ford R1114	Plaxton Supreme III	C45DL	1977	
MIB268	Ford R1014	Plaxton Supreme III	C45F	1977	Ex North Mymms Coaches, 1984
MIB278	Leyland Leopard PSU3E/4R	Duple Dominant I	C49F	1977	Ex Stoniers, Newcastle, 1992
MIB783	Ford R1114	Plaxton Supreme III	C53F	1977	Ex Price, Shareshill, 1984
MIB270	Ford R1114	Plaxton Supreme IV Express	C53F	1979	Ex Rochdale Borough Council, 1990
MIB537	Leyland Leopard PSU5C/4R	Plaxton Supreme IV	C57F	1979	Ex Marinair, Canterbury, 1989
MIB279	Leyland Tiger TRCTL11/3R	Plaxton Paramount 3200 E	C53F	1983	Ex Wessex, Bristol, 1991
MIB346	Leyland Tiger TRCTL11/3R	Plaxton Paramount 3200 E	C57F	1983	Ex Wessex, Bristol, 1991
MIB614	Leyland Tiger TRCTL11/3R	Plaxton Paramount 3200 E	C50FT	1983	Ex Wessex, Bristol, 1991
MIB516	DAF MB200DKFL600	Plaxton Paramount 3500	C51F	1983	Ex Lewis, Pailton, 1989
MIB864	DAF MB200DKTL600	Jonckheere Bermuda	C32FT	1983	Ex Slatepearl, Trentham, 1985
MIB536	Leyland Tiger TRCTL11/3R	Plaxton Paramount 3200	C57F	1983	Ex Hazeldine, Bilston, 1988
MIB615	DAF MB200DKFL600	Plaxton Paramount 3200	C42FTL	1984	Ex Kinch, Montsorrel, 1988
MIB246	Leyland Tiger TRCTL11/3R	Plaxton Paramount 3500	C53F	1985	
MIB746	Renault-Dodge S56	Reeve Burgess Beaver	B23F	1986	Ex Sherratt, Cold Meece, 1993
MIB293	Renault-Dodge S56	Reeve Burgess Beaver	B23F	1986	Ex Sherratt, Cold Meece, 1993
MIB905	Renault-Dodge S56	Northern Counties	B18F	1986	Ex Sherratt, Cold Meece, 1993
MIB970	Mercedes-Benz 811D	North West CS	C21F	1987	Ex Grant, Aintree, 1989
MIB302	Leyland Royal Tiger RTC	Leyland Doyen	C49F	1987	Ex Kingsman, Matlock, 1990
MIB236	Leyland Tiger TRCL10/3ARZM	Plaxton Paramount 3500 III	C53FT	1988	Ex Volvo demonstrator, 1990
MIB761	Toyota Coaster HB31R	Caetano Optimo	C21F	1989	Ex Kinch, Barrow-on-Soar, 1993

Previous Registrations:

MIB236	F683SRN	MIB536	A669HNX
MIB246	B888SEH	MIB537	DDG266T
MIB268	SEL119R, 292MVT	MIB614	EAH892Y, CIW6752, FFA270Y
MIB270	EYG524T	MIB615	A102HJF
MIB278	YTU321S	MIB746	D157LTA
MIB279	EAH889Y, CIW1939, FFA301Y	MIB761	G860WBC
MIB293	D167LTA	MIB783	UUX388S
MIB302	D813SET	MIB864	YRF754Y, 470WYA
MIB346	EAH893Y, CIW9721, FFA271Y	MIB905	C804CBU
MIB516	EFK135Y	MIB970	D84OVM
MIB520	TRE202R, 111WEH		

Livery: Blue, black and red

Copeland's recent commercial services operate from Longton, though they have been operating tendered services for some time. Seen shortly after joining the Meir-based fleet, and on one of these services is D157LTA, a Renault-Dodge S56 originating from the batch delivered to Plymouth in 1986. It has since been re-registered MIB746 allowing the fleet to retain 100% private number record.
Graham Ashworth

DOBSON'S

R E Dobson, Mountbatten Fields, 242 Manchester Road, Lostock Gralam,
Northwich, Cheshire, CW9 7PL

J332FVM	Peugeot-Talbot Pullman	Talbot	B22F	1991
J387PVR	Peugeot-Talbot Pullman	TBP	B22F	1992
L483DOA	Peugeot-Talbot Pullman	TBP	B22F	1993

Livery: White

Dobson's operate the tri-axle minibus from Peugeot-Talbot, known in its bus form as the Pullman.
With the rear lift in place, and with other suitable modification, is marketed as the Freeway. G701RNE,
seen working a Cheshire Bus service in Watling Street, Northwich, is typical of the type, though this
vehicle has recently been replaced by a similar model. *Graham Ashworth*

ELCOCK REISEN

M H Elcock & Son Ltd, The Maddocks, Madeley, Telford, Shropshire, TF7 5HA

Depots: The Maddocks, Telford; Admaston Road, Wellington.

TNT383S	Ford R1114	Plaxton Supreme III	C53F	1977	Ex Brown, Telford, 1992
WAW356S	Ford R1114	Plaxton Supreme III	C53F	1978	Ex Shropshire Education, 1990
ATH4V	Ford R1114	Plaxton Supreme IV	C53F	1979	Ex Castle Garage, Llandovery, 1989
HUJ998V	Ford R1114	Plaxton Supreme IV	C53F	1980	
HUJ999V	Ford R1114	Plaxton Supreme IV	C53F	1980	
JAW84V	Ford R1114	Plaxton Supreme IV	C53F	1980	Ex Excelsior, Telford, 1984
1577NT	Volvo B10M-61	Plaxton Paramount 3500 II	C53F	1986	Ex Clarke, London, 1992
E222WUX	Volvo B10M-61	Plaxton Paramount 3200 III	C53F	1988	
E961YUX	Ford Transit VE6	Ford	M15	1988	
E666YAW	Mercedes-Benz 709D	Reeve Burgess	C25F	1988	
F39GAW	Mercedes-Benz 709D	Crystals	C24F	1988	Ex Dave Parry, Cheslyn Hay, 1990
3408NT	Volvo B10M-61	Plaxton Paramount 3500 III	C49FT	1988	
3572NT	DAF MB230LB615	Plaxton Paramount 3500 III	C51F	1988	
F482WFX	Mercedes-Benz 811D	Reeve Burgess Beaver	C29F	1989	Ex Excelsior, Bournemouth, 1992
EIL829	Volvo B10M-60	Plaxton Paramount 3200 III	C53FT	1989	Ex Excelsior, Bournemouth, 1993
EIL1607	Volvo B10M-60	Plaxton Paramount 3200 III	C53FT	1989	Ex Excelsior, Bournemouth, 1993
5038NT	Volvo B10M-60	Plaxton Paramount 3500 III	C53FT	1989	Ex Parks, Hamilton, 1991
HIL6584	Volvo B10M-60	Plaxton Paramount 3500 III	C53FT	1989	Ex Parks, Hamilton, 1991
G555JAW	DAF MB230LB615	Plaxton Paramount 3500 III	C51F	1990	
G444JAW	Mercedes-Benz 811D	Reeve Burgess Beaver	C25F	1989	
G333JUX	Volvo B10M-60	Plaxton Paramount 3500 III	C49FT	1989	
1398NT	Volvo B10M-60	Plaxton Paramount 3500 III	C49FT	1990	Ex Parks, Hamilton, 1991
EIL2247	Volvo B10M-60	Plaxton Paramount 3500 III	C49FT	1990	Ex Parks, Hamilton, 1991
J921UUX	Mercedes-Benz 709D	Europa	C24F	1991	
K321AUX	Volvo B10M-60	Jonckheere Deauville P599	C49FT	1992	
K123CAW	Volvo B10M-60	Jonckheere Deauville P599	C49FT	1993	
L321JUJ	Volvo B10M-60	Plaxton Premiére 350	C49FT	1994	

Previous Registrations:

1398NT	G59RGG	EIL1607	F462WFX, XEL158, F769MAA
1577NT	C177LWB	EIL2247	G87RGG
3408NT	F555CAW	EIL829	F461WFX, XEL31, XEL24, F755MAA
3572NT	From new	F39GAW	F201LPD, 3408NT
5038NT	F985HGE	HIL6584	F966HGE

Livery: Silver, red and gold.

Elcock Reisen operate a high specification coach fleet with most of its work concentrated on continental and British extended tours and private hire, especially to the Germanic countries. Coaches purchased new have a high specification. Illustrated here is F555CAW, of the higher-floor Paramount 3500 type, its age now disguised to the unwary through a recent re-registration.
John Jones

While back at Telford, the tour coaches from the Elcock fleet augment the Fords on Shropshire Bus tendered work and contracts. A pair of DAF MB230s were purchased in 1989-90, and the first of these, 3572NT is seen in Wellington. *Bill Potter*

Two of the Jonckheere Deauville P599 were purchased for use on the continental tours and K123CAW is seen at the new Wellington depot after being prepared for a ski-tour to Austria in February 1994. Doubtless the essential snow-chains are packed ready to use in the lockers. The new depot is on the former Philjo site and has replaced the Ironbridge location and a small unit in Dawley, and while the Madely site will be retained, the offices are expected to move to Wellington shortly. *Bill Potter*

FRONTLINE

Frontline Enterprises Ltd, Birch Coppice, Dordon, Staffordshire, B78 1TA

A member of Badgerline Group plc

RM471	KVS601	AEC Routemaster 5RM	Park Royal	H36/28R	1961	Ex Kelvin Scottish, 1993
1929	MHJ725V	Leyland National 2 NL116L11/1R		B49F	1980	Ex Eastern National, 1993
1931	MHJ727V	Leyland National 2 NL116L11/1R		B49F	1980	Ex Eastern National, 1993
1937	STW18W	Leyland National 2 NL116L11/1R		B49F	1980	Ex Eastern National, 1993
5021	L21AHA	Mercedes-Benz 709D	Plaxton Beaver	B23F	1993	
5755	D755RWC	Ford Transit 190	Dormobile	B16F	1986	Ex Thamesway, 1993
6448	NOC448R	Leyland Fleetline FE30AGR	MCW	H43/33F	1977	Ex Midland Fox, 1992
6525	SDA525S	Leyland Fleetline FE30AGR	MCW	H43/33F	1977	Ex Burman, Tamworth, 1992
6726	NOC726R	Leyland Fleetline FE30AGR	East Lancashire	H43/33F	1977	Ex C & M, Aintree, 1992
8145	PCK145P	Leyland Leopard PSU3C/4R	Duple Dominant	C53F	1975	Ex Burman, Tamworth, 1992
8216	DAK216V	Leyland Leopard PSU5C/4R	Duple Dominant II	C50F	1980	Ex Burman, Tamworth, 1992
8322	BJT322T	Leyland Leopard PSU3E/4R	Plaxton Supreme IV Express	C49F	1979	Ex Burman, Tamworth, 1992
8811	VJG811T	Leyland Leopard PSU3E/4RT	Duple Dominant II	C53F	1979	Ex Burman, Tamworth, 1992
8822	OKY822X	Leyland Leopard PSU5C/4R	Plaxton Supreme VI Express	C57F	1982	Ex Burman, Tamworth, 1992
8953	YSU953	Leyland Tiger TRCTL11/3RH	Plaxton Paramount 3200 E	C53F	1983	Ex Burman, Tamworth, 1992
8954	YSU954	Leyland Tiger TRCTL11/3RH	Plaxton Paramount 3200 E	C53F	1983	Ex Burman, Tamworth, 1992

Previous Registrations:

KVS601	WLT471, EDS394A	YSU954	A622ATV
YSU953	A618ATV		

Livery: Red and gold

Frontline of Dordon near Tamworth, is a subsidiary of the Badgerline group with a good variety of vehicles in this small fleet. KVS601 is a former London Buses AEC Routemaster which came to Frontline from Kelvin Scottish. It was RM471 with London Transport, which number it retains with Frontline on a livery not vastly different from the one originally worn in London.
Tim Weatherup

There are three Leyland Nationals in the Frontline Buses fleet and MHJ725V is a Leyland National 2 that came from Eastern National, in company with two others, in 1993. It is turning into the terminal point for service 789 in Tamworth town centre. *Colin Lloyd*

There are only two minibuses in the Frontline fleet - a Ford Transit and this new Mercedes-Benz 709D with Plaxton bodywork. Although not visible in this picture L21AHA carries fleet number 5021. It was diverted from an Eastern National order in August 1993, and was the first Frontline vehicle to carry the Badger logo. It is seen here in Aldergate, Tamworth.
Colin Lloyd

Duple Dominant II Express bodywork is carried by this 1979 Leyland Leopard, VJG811T. It started life in the East Kent fleet before passing to Burman of Mile Oak. That concern moved to Dordon and was taken over by Frontline in August 1992. Burman had originally re-painted this vehicle into National Express livery though, as far as is known, it did not run on National Express work for them.
Colin Lloyd

Much of Frontline's double-deck operations are performed by three Daimler Fleetlines, two with MCW bodywork, the third with an East Lancashire product. All were new to West Midlands PTE as examples of their standard vehicle. No.6448, NOC448R, is seen in Birmingham city centre.
Graham Ashworth

Green Bus operate many Leyland Leopards on their services which serve the communities throughout south Staffordshire and into Wolverhampton. It is in this town where, recently withdrawn 22, ETC665J, is seen entering the bus station.

Green Bus Service have, for many years, operated a fleet of elderly vehicles in immaculate livery and condition. One of the newer vehicles in the fleet is 13, GHB20N, which was acquired from Blue Bus of Horwich in July 1992. It continues a long history of operating Leyland Leopards. Plaxton Derwent bodywork is fitted and the vehicle was new in 1974 to Hills of Tredegar. *Graham Ashworth*

GREEN BUS SERVICE

Warstone Motors Ltd, The Garage, Jacobs Hall Lane, Great Wyrley,
Staffordshire, WS6 6AD

1	WTJ901L	Leyland Leopard PSU4B/2R	East Lancashire	B45F	1972	Ex Rossendale, 1988
2	DDW65V	Leyland Leopard PSU4E/2R	East Lancashire	B45F	1979	Ex Stevensons, 1993
3	WTJ903L	Leyland Leopard PSU4B/2R	East Lancashire	B45F	1972	Ex Rossendale, 1988
4	RWU535R	Leyland Leopard PSU4D/4R	Plaxton Derwent	B46F	1976	Ex Stuarts, Hyde, 1993
5	WTJ905L	Leyland Leopard PSU4B/2R	East Lancashire	B45F	1972	Ex Rossendale, 1988
6	RWT527R	Leyland Leopard PSU4D/4R	Plaxton Derwent	B43F	1976	Ex Rider York, 1992
7	RWT531R	Leyland Leopard PSU4D/4R	Plaxton Derwent	B47F	1976	Ex Rider York, 1992
8	XWG628T	Leyland Atlantean AN68A/1R	Roe	H45/29D	1978	Ex Trans Manche Link, Folkestone, 1993
9	UET678S	Leyland Atlantean AN68A/1R	Alexander AL	H45/29D	1978	Ex South Yorkshire, 1990
10	RFR410P	Leyland Atlantean AN68/1R	Eastern Coach Works	H43/31F	1976	Ex Ribble, 1993
11	WVM893S	Leyland Atlantean AN68A/1R	Park Royal	H43/32F	1972	Ex G M Buses, 1991
12	GNY432C	Leyland Titan PD3/4	Massey	L33/35RD	1965	Ex Rhymney Valley, 1981
13	GHB20N	Leyland Leopard PSU4B/2R	Plaxton Derwent	B47F	1974	Ex Blue Bus, Horwich, 1992
14	RWT529R	Leyland Leopard PSU4D/4R	Plaxton Derwent	B43F	1976	Ex Stuarts, Hyde, 1993
15	GCA747	Bedford OB	Duple Vista	C29F	1950	Ex Sargeant, Llanfaredd, 1973
16	MTC870K	Leyland Leopard PSU4B/2R	East Lancashire	B46F	1972	Ex Rossendale, 1989
17	NTX576R	Leyland Leopard PSU4C/2R	Willowbrook	B45F	1977	Ex Phil Anslow, Garndiffaith, 1992
18	MTC868K	Leyland Leopard PSU4B/2R	East Lancashire	B46F	1972	Ex Rossendale, 1989
19	DUH77V	Leyland Leopard PSU3E/2R	East Lancashire	B47F	1979	Ex Stevensons, 1993
20	RWT528R	Leyland Leopard PSU4D/4R	Plaxton Derwent	B43F	1976	Ex Parkinson, Allerton Bywater, 1993
21	DUH76V	Leyland Leopard PSU3E/2R	East Lancashire	B47F	1980	Ex Stevensons, 1993
22	DUH78V	Leyland Leopard PSU3E/2R	East Lancashire	B47F	1979	Ex Stevensons, 1993
23	YBO17T	Leyland Leopard PSU3E/2R	East Lancashire	B51F	1979	Ex Parfitts, Rhymney Bridge, 1994
24	HTF179K	Leyland Atlantean PDR1A/1	East Lancashire	H45/33F	1971	Ex Rossendale, 1988

Livery: Green, cream and yellow

**Green Bus Services'
double-deck
requirement is met
by the Leyland
Atlantean, with all
four AN68s carrying
different makes of
bodywork. From the
Roe factory is 8,
XWG628T. It arrived
in Great Wyrley after
service with the
Channel Tunnel
construction
consortium.**
Graham Ashworth

HALTON

Halton Borough Transport Ltd, Moor Lane, Widnes, Cheshire, WA8 7AF

2	MDL880R	Leyland National 11351A/1R		B52F	1976	Ex Southern Vectis, 1987
3	ODL884R	Leyland National 10351A/1R		B44F	1977	Ex Southern Vectis, 1987
4	ODL883R	Leyland National 10351A/1R		B44F	1977	Ex Southern Vectis, 1987
8	F687YWM	Leyland Lynx LX112L10ZR1	Leyland Lynx	B51F	1988	
9	F81STB	Leyland Lynx LX112L10ZR1	Leyland Lynx	B51F	1989	
11	H34HBG	Leyland Lynx LX2R11C15Z4R	Leyland Lynx	B51F	1991	
13	YTU983S	Leyland National 11351A/1R		B49F	1977	Ex Crosville, 1987
14	F520AEM	Leyland Lynx LX112L10ZR1	Leyland Lynx	B51F	1989	
15	F521AEM	Leyland Lynx LX112L10ZR1	Leyland Lynx	B51F	1989	
16	F895BKF	Leyland Lynx LX112L10ZR1	Leyland Lynx	B51F	1989	
17	G221DKA	Leyland Lynx LX2R11C15Z4S	Leyland Lynx	B51F	1989	
19	ACW919R	Leyland National 11351A/2R		B52F	1977	
21	ACW921R	Leyland National 11351A/2R		B52F	1977	
22	BTB22T	Leyland National 11351A/1R		B52F	1979	
23	BTB23T	Leyland National 11351A/1R		B52F	1979	
24	BTB24T	Leyland National 11351A/1R		B52F	1979	
25	HED203V	Leyland National NL116L11/1R		B52F	1980	
26	G222DKA	Leyland Lynx LX2R11C15Z4R	Leyland Lynx	B51F	1989	
27	G474DHF	Leyland Lynx LX2R11C15Z4R	Leyland Lynx	B51F	1990	
28	CKC928X	Leyland National 2 NL116AL11/1R		B52F	1982	
29	CKC929X	Leyland National 2 NL116AL11/1R		B52F	1982	
30	EWM630Y	Leyland National 2 NL116TL11/1R		B52F	1983	
31	B131SED	Leyland National 2 NL116TL11/1R		B52F	1985	
32	B132SED	Leyland National 2 NL116TL11/1R		B52F	1985	
33	C49OCM	Leyland National 2 NL116TL11/1R		B52F	1985	
34	D711SKB	Leyland Lynx LX563TL11FR1	Leyland Lynx	B51F	1986	
35	H35HBG	Leyland Lynx LX2R11C15Z4R	Leyland Lynx II	B51F	1990	
36	J249KWM	Leyland Lynx LX2R11C15Z4R	Leyland Lynx II	B51F	1991	
37	J250KWM	Leyland Lynx LX112L10ZR1R	Leyland	B51F	1991	
38	J251KWM	Leyland Lynx LX2R11C15Z4R	Leyland Lynx II	B51F	1991	
39	ODL887R	Leyland National 10351A-1R		B44F	1977	Ex Southern Vectis, 1987
40	ODL886R	Leyland National 10351A-1R		B44F	1977	Ex Southern Vectis, 1987
43	E641VFY	Leyland Lynx LX112TL11ZR1R	Leyland Lynx	B51F	1987	
44	E49WEM	Leyland Lynx LX112L10ZR1	Leyland Lynx	B51F	1988	
45	E642VFY	Leyland Lynx LX112L10ZR1	Leyland Lynx	B51F	1988	
46	J628LHF	Leyland Lynx LX2R11C15Z4S	Leyland Lynx II	B51F	1992	
47	J630LHF	Leyland Lynx LX2R11C15Z4S	Leyland Lynx II	B51F	1992	
48	J629LHF	Leyland Lynx LX2R11C15Z4S	Leyland Lynx II	B51F	1992	
49	J929MKC	Leyland Lynx LX2R11C15Z4S	Leyland Lynx II	B51F	1992	
50	H543FWM	Leyland Lynx LX2R11C15Z4R	Leyland Lynx II	B51F	1990	
51	H544FWM	Leyland Lynx LX2R11C15Z4R	Leyland Lynx II	B51F	1990	
52	J925MKC	Leyland Lynx LX2R11C15Z4R	Leyland Lynx II	B51F	1992	
53	K852MTJ	Leyland Lynx LX2R11C15Z4S	Leyland Lynx II	B51F	1992	
54	G473DHF	Leyland Lynx LX2R11C15Z4R	Leyland Lynx	B51F	1990	
55	G803EKA	Leyland Lynx LX2R11C15Z4R	Leyland Lynx	B51F	1990	
56	H542FWM	Leyland Lynx LX2R11C15Z4R	Leyland Lynx	B51F	1990	
57	K853MTJ	Leyland Lynx LX2R11C15Z4S	Leyland Lynx II	B51F	1992	
58	J921MKC	Leyland Lynx LX2R11C15Z4S	Leyland Lynx II	B51F	1992	
59	J922MKC	Leyland Lynx LX2R11C15Z4S	Leyland Lynx II	B51F	1992	
60	J923MKC	Leyland Lynx LX2R11C15Z4S	Leyland Lynx II	B51F	1992	
61	J924MKC	Leyland Lynx LX2R11C15Z4S	Leyland Lynx II	B51F	1992	
62	J926MKC	Leyland Lynx LX2R11C15Z4S	Leyland Lynx II	B51F	1992	
63	J927MKC	Leyland Lynx LX2R11C15Z4S	Leyland Lynx II	B51F	1992	
64	J928MKC	Leyland Lynx LX2R11C15Z4S	Leyland Lynx II	B51F	1992	

Halton have been keen purchasers of the Leyland National and its successor, the Lynx, with many of the first and last of each entering the fleet. No. 54, G473DHF, a 1990 Leyland Lynx is typical of the early models and is seen returning to the depot on a visit made by the Ribble Enthusists' Club. *Bill Potter*

While the Leyland National was of integral construction, the Lynx had a clearly defined chassis. Minor body style differences hide the significant engineering enhancements introduced with the Lynx II and Halton 50, H543FWM, is one of these. A somewhat larger quantity than usual was ordered when Volvo announced the closure of the Lynx production line. *Malc McDonald*

HALTON MINI COACHES

S Williams, 106 Main Street, Halton Village, Runcorn, Cheshire, WA7 2PW

E538YKO	Peugeot-Talbot Pullman	Talbot	DP20F	1988	Ex Dobsons, Lostock Gralam, 1993
E653OCW	Peugeot-Talbot Pullman	Talbot	B22F	1988	Ex Dobsons, Lostock Gralam, 1993
G966SND	Mazda E2200	Made-to-Measure	M14	1990	
G366UVR	Peugeot-Talbot Express	Made-to-Measure	M14	1990	
H233BBA	Peugeot-Talbot Pullman	Talbot	B22F	1991	Ex Dobson, Lostock Gralam, 1992
H14JYM	Mercedes-Benz 609D	Whittaker	B19F	1991	Ex Jim Stones, Glazebury, 1992
L5HMC	Leyland DAF 400	Leyland DAF	M16	1993	

Livery: Silver with black relief

Halton Mini Coaches provide minibus services around the Runcorn area and also operate on the busway. However, H14JYM is seen many miles away from the area, at York races, while working a private hire. *Graham Ashworth*

HANDYBUS

A J Matthews, Marsh Tree Garage, Hassall Street, Newcastle-under-Lyme,
Staffordshire, ST5 1BB

VRF660S	Ford Transit 160	Deansgate	M12	1977	Ex Morris, Loggerheads, 1993
B413NJF	Ford Transit 190	Rootes	B16F	1985	Ex Irwell Valley, Boothstown, 1992
B414NJF	Ford Transit 190	Rootes	B16F	1985	Ex Irwell Valley, Boothstown, 1992
B422NJF	Ford Transit 190	Rootes	B16F	1985	Ex Stoniers, 1993
C576TUT	Ford Transit 190	Dormobile	B16F	1986	Ex Stevensons, 1992
D122WCC	Freight Rover Sherpa	Carlyle	B18F	1987	Ex Stoniers, 1993
D113TFT	Freight Rover Sherpa	Carlyle	B18F	1987	Ex Stoniers, 1993

Livery: Blue and red

The Handybus minibus operation includes some vehicles which retain the Matthews Motors name. The most numerous type in the fleet is the Ford Transit and B413NJF is one of three now re-united from the same batch. It is seen in Newcastle bus station. *Graham Ashworth*

HAPPY DAYS

Happy Days (Woodseaves) Ltd, Knightley Gorse Garage, Woodseaves,
Staffordshire, ST20 0JR

117	MOD573P	Bristol VRT/SL3/6LXB	Eastern Coach Works	H43/32F	1976	Ex Yelloway, Rochdale, 1989
118	OUP677P	Bristol VRT/SL3/6LXB	Eastern Coach Works	H43/31F	1976	Ex Yelloway, Rochdale, 1989
119	UNW929R	Bristol VRT/SL3/6LXB	Eastern Coach Works	H43/31F	1977	Ex Happy Al's, Birkenhead, 1993
120	RYG385R	Bristol VRT/SL3/6LXB	Eastern Coach Works	H43/31F	1976	Ex Happy Al's, Birkenhead, 1993
121	RYG389R	Bristol VRT/SL3/6LXB	Eastern Coach Works	H43/31F	1976	Ex Happy Al's, Birkenhead, 1993
122	WDM352R	Bristol VRT/SL3/501	Eastern Coach Works	H43/31F	1977	Ex PMT, 1992
137	DEC578S	Volvo B58-61	Duple Dominant II	C57F	1977	Ex Shaw-Hadwin, Silverdale, 1992
138	ARF989T	Volvo B58-56	Duple Dominant II	C53F	1979	Ex Wallace Arnold, 1985
146	XWC18	Volvo B10M-61	Duple Dominant IV	C53F	1982	Ex Aintree Coachline, 1992
175	917DBO	Volvo B10M-60	Plaxton Paramount 3500 III	C49FT	1989	
178	G779CFA	Scania K113CRB	Van Hool Alizée	C49FT	1990	
181	K1HDC	Scania K113CRB	Van Hool Alizée	C48FT	1993	
182	K11HDC	Scania K113CRB	Van Hool Alizée	C48FT	1993	
183	L4WOL	Volvo B10M-60	Plaxton Excalibur	C38FT	1993	
185	L1HDC	Volvo B10M-60	Jonckheere Deauville P599	C51FT	1993	

Previous Registrations:

917DBO	F362URF	WHA325	G554CRF
ARF989T	EWW227T, XWC18	XWC18	WVT887X
DEC578S	CHG310S, 525XPD		

Livery: White, red and black.

Latest arrival in the Happy Days fleet is L1HDC, a Volvo B10M and the first in the fleet with Jonckheere Deauville bodywork. Happy Days are just one of several operators who, in recent years, have choosen to place the DVLA Select marks on their vehicles. *Graham Ashworth*

Happy Days have recently reduced the size of their fleet, a casualty being 170, 18XWC, a Auwaerter Neoplan Skyliner, a double-deck coach. *Philip Stephenson*

Happy Days provide vehicles for National Express relief work and 178, G779CFA, is seen so employed, turning into Buckingham Palace Road, London. Based on a Scania K113 it is one of three similar vehicles currently in the fleet where, in recent years both Swedish manufacturing giants have tussled for supremacy. *Colin Lloyd*

HORROCKS

A P Horrocks, Ivy House, Brockton, Lydbury North, Shropshire, SY7 8BA

GAX2C	Bristol RELL6G	Eastern Coach Works	B54F	1965	Ex Wood, Craven Arms, 1992
VOD545K	Bristol VRT/SL2/6G	Eastern Coach Works	H39/31F	1971	Ex Wood, Craven Arms, 1992
CDC168K	Seddon Pennine 7	Plaxton Elite III	C45F	1972	Ex Trefaldwyn, Montgomery, 1989
PGX235L	Ford R192	Willowbrook 001	DP43F	1973	Ex Cunningham, Stanford-le-Hope, 1990
GWP633N	Bedford YRT	Duple Dominant	C53F	1975	Ex Trefaldwyn, Montgomery, 1989
TTT236R	Bedford YMT	Duple Dominant II	C53F	1977	Ex Trefaldwyn, Montgomery, 1989
DJF633T	Bedford YMT	Plaxton Supreme IV	C53F	1979	Ex Jones, Annscroft, 1991
D625BCK	Iveco Daily 49.10	Robin Hood City Nippy	B25F	1987	Ex Ribble, 1993
D261OOJ	Freight Rover Sherpa	Carlyle	B18F	1987	Ex King Offa, Westbury, 1993

Livery: White

On a base of white, the Horrocks name is painted in large multi-colour letters in (almost) reverse-rainbow order. DJF633T arrived with Horrocks shortly after Mr Horrocks moved from the South Wales Traffic Area where he had taken over the remains of the Trefaldwyn business.
Graham Ashworth

HUXLEY

J F Huxley, Rose Cottage, Greaves Lane East, Threapwood, Malpas,
Cheshire, SY14 7AT

JDT344N	Leyland National 10351/2R		B40D	1975	Ex Orion, Kirkaldy, 1994
LWO735P	Ford R1114	Duple Dominant	C53F	1976	Ex Humphries, Bridgend, 1979
SPC274R	Leyland National 10351A/1R		B41F	1977	Ex Northumbria, 1993
UTO3S	Ford R1114	Plaxton Supreme III	C49F	1977	Ex Parish, Hawarden, 1987
YGD767S	Ford R1114	Duple Dominant	C53F	1978	Ex Stevens, West Bromwich, 1991
YWO182	Ford R1114	Plaxton Supreme III	C40FT	1978	Ex Bee-Line, Middlesbrough, 1983
HIL3931	Ford R1114	Plaxton Supreme III Express	C53F	1978	
HIL3934	Leyland Leopard PSU3E/4R	Duple Dominant I	C49F	1978	Ex Pride of the Road, Royston, 1990
HIL3935	Leyland Leopard PSU3E/4R	Duple Dominant I	C49F	1978	Ex Pride of the Road, Royston, 1990
HIL3932	Leyland Leopard PSU5C/4R	Duple Dominant I	C53F	1979	Ex Yorkshire Rider, 1991
FUJ937V	Bedford YMT	Duple Dominant II	C53F	1980	Ex Smith, Amble, 1991
YBN632V	Leyland Leopard PSU3E/4R	Plaxton Supreme IV Express	C51F	1980	Ex Aintree Coachline, 1992
ESK879	Volvo B10M-61	Van Hool Alizée	C52F	1982	Ex Appleby, Conisholme, 1991
MFE504	Volvo B10M-61	Van Hool Alizée	C46FT	1982	Ex Tellings, Byfleet, 1988
HOI2804	DAF MB200DKFL600	Van Hool Alizée	C50FT	1983	Ex Eniway, Dereham, 1989
PMB142Y	Dennis Falcon V SDA404	Duple Goldliner IV	C53F	1983	Ex Parish, Hawarden, 1987
ESK882	Bova EL26/581	Bova Europa	C53F	1984	Ex County, Leicester, 1990
B319RJF	Bova EL26/581	Bova Europa	C53F	1984	Ex County, Leicester, 1990
D120WCC	Freight Rover Sherpa	Carlyle	B18F	1987	Ex Amberline, 1992

Previous Registrations:

B319RJF	B245YKX, 5946PP	HIL3935	PVB807S
ESK879	VAT222W, AAG275X	HOI2804	KOO760Y
ESK882	B252YKX, 625PP, B291RJF	JDT433N	JDT433N, 2749MAN
HIL3931	DDM11S	MFE504	From new
HIL3932	BWE197T	PMB142Y	ANA100Y
HIL3934	PVB806S	YWO182	UUX385S

Livery: Yellow and white or brown and cream.

Penyffordd is a village on the Chester to Wrexham 'back roads' service which is one of many in the area served by Huxley on behalf of Cheshire Bus. HIL3934 is one of three Duple Dominant Is, the express-doored variant produced for the National Bus Company and Scottish Bus Group.
Graham Ashworth

JONES

Jones Coachways Ltd, 20a Shropshire Street, Market Drayton, Shropshire, TF9 3BY

150	XWJ791T	Ford R1114	Plaxton Supreme III	C53F	1979	Ex Finsbury, London EC1, 1979
152	JFD296V	Ford R1114	Duple Dominant II	C53F	1979	Ex Olsen, Strood, 1981
155	RAW735X	Ford R1114	Duple Dominant II	C53F	1982	
158	A531CUX	Mercedes-Benz L608D	Reeve Burgess	C21F	1984	
159	B250HUX	Ford R1115	Plaxton Paramount 3200 II	C53F	1985	
161	JNK984N	Ford R1114	Plaxton Elite III	C53F	1975	Ex Goode, West Bromwich, 1985
162	BLJ720Y	Ford R1115	Plaxton Paramount 3200	C53F	1983	Ex Excelsior, Bournemouth, 1986
164	D720TNT	Volvo B10M-61	Plaxton Paramount 3500 III	C53F	1987	
165	WNR606S	Ford R1114	Duple Dominant II	C53F	1978	Ex Greenway Travel, Hitchin, 1990
166	G587LUX	Mercedes-Benz 811D	Reeve Burgess Beaver	C25F	1990	
167	G529MNT	Dennis Javelin 12SDA1907	Duple 320	C57F	1990	
168	F907UPR	Dennis Javelin 12SDA1907	Plaxton Paramount 3200 III	C51FT	1989	Ex Goldline, Wimbourne, 1991
169	G92RGG	Volvo B10M-60	Plaxton Paramount 3500 III	C53F	1990	Ex Parks, Hamilton, 1993
170	NLC871V	Volvo B58-61	Plaxton Supreme IV	C51F	1980	Ex Seaview, Parkstone, 1992
171	EDF274T	Leyland Leopard PSU5C/4R	Plaxton Supreme IV	C57F	1979	Ex Spring, Evesham, 1993
172	G93RGG	Volvo B10M-60	Plaxton Paramount 3500 III	C53F	1990	Ex Parks, Hamilton, 1993
173	J436HDS	Volvo B10M-60	Plaxton Premiére 350	C53F	1992	Ex Parks, Hamilton, 1993

Livery: Blue/grey and brown.

Photographed as it left Nantwich for Crewe on the company's Saturday-only Market Drayton service is Jones 162, BLJ720Y, a Ford R1115 with Plaxton Paramount 3200 bodywork. The R1115, essentially a re-engined R114, did not sell in large numbers - the decline in Ford's popularity already unstopable. *Graham Ashworth*

KING OFFA TRAVEL

King Offa Travel Services Ltd, The Lodge, Winsley Hall, Westbury,
Shropshire, SY5 9HB

DNT527T	Leyland Leopard PSU3E/4R	Plaxton Supreme III Express	C51F	1978	Ex Midland Red North, 1990
WOC739T	Leyland Leopard PSU3E/4R	Plaxton Supreme III Express	C49F	1979	Ex Midland Red North, 1992
LVS433V	Bedford YMT	Plaxton Supreme IV	C53F	1980	Ex Linkfast, Hadleigh, 1993
DDM22X	Leyland Leopard PSU3F/4R	Willowbrook 003	C53F	1981	Ex Grimsby Cleethorpes, 1994
HKP126	Leyland Tiger TRCTL11/3R	Plaxton Paramount 3500	C50F	1983	Ex Drawlane, 1991
A101JJT	Leyland Tiger TRCTL11/3R	Plaxton Paramount 3200	C57F	1984	Ex Midland Red North, 1992

Previous Registrations:

DNT527T	APR818T, HKP126	HKP126	BRN4Y

Livery: White, blue and red.

A101JJT, a Leyland Tiger with Plaxton Paramount 3200 bodywork is one of several vehicles now in the King Offa Travel fleet that originated from Midland Red North. It was photogrpahed at Rothersthorpe Services on the M1 motorway which, as all collectors of trivia know, is one of only two service areas run by Blue Boar! *Graham Ashworth*

KNOTTY

MA & SM Hearson, Unit C, Parkhouse Road East, Parkhouse Industrial Estate, Chesterton, Newcastle, Staffordshire, ST5 7RB

2	PPH431R	AEC Reliance 6U3ZR	Plaxton Supreme III Express	C53F	1977	Ex LMS Travel, Chesterton, 1991
3	KVE909P	AEC Reliance 6U3ZR	Plaxton Supreme III Express	C49F	1975	Ex Premier, Cambridge, 1988
6	JWO891L	AEC Reliance 6MU4R	Plaxton Elite III Express	C51F	1973	Ex Hall, Rock End, 1989
9	UAD316H	Daimler Roadliner SRP8	Plaxton Elite	C47F	1970	Ex Offerton Coaches, Stockport, 1989
10	TPD12S	AEC Reliance 6U2R	Plaxton Supreme III	C53F	1978	Ex Happy Times, Wednesfield, 1990
12	KGR258T	AEC Reliance 6U2R	Duple Dominant II	C55F	1978	Ex Marshall, Sutton-on-Trent, 1990
14	ANA8T	AEC Reliance 6U3ZR	Plaxton Supreme III	C53F	1978	Ex Lancaster, 1991
16	GEM598N	AEC Swift 3MP2R	Marshall	B42D	1974	Ex Archer Travel, Liverpool, 1991
17	JPA171K	AEC Reliance 6U2R	Park Royal	B49F	1972	Ex Buffalo, Flitwick, 1992
19	CYA181J	AEC Reliance 6MU3R	Plaxton Derwent	B47F	1971	Ex Chiltern Queens, Woodcote, 1992
20	OFR983M	AEC Swift 3MP2R	Marshall	B47D	1974	Ex Wealden Beeline, 1993
21	MWA839P	AEC Reliance 6U3ZR	Plaxton Supreme III	C53F	1976	Ex Fallon, Dunbar, 1993
22	VCW598Y	Dennis Lancet SD505	Marshall Camair 80	B51F	1982	Ex Redby Travel, Sunderland, 1993
23	JPF103K	AEC Swift 3MP2R	Alexander W	DP45F	1972	Ex Blue Triangle, Bootle, 1993
24	EDJ242J	AEC Swift 3MP2R	Marshall	B44D	1971	Ex preservation, 1994
25	NKN101M	AEC Reliance 6U3ZR	Plaxton Elite III	C53F	1976	Ex Davies, Hawkhurst, 1994

Livery: White, grey, black and red.

One of that rare breed, the rear-engined Daimler Roadliner, UAD316H is still to be found in the Knotty fleet. Subject to recent controversy in the pages of that excellent journal 'Classic Bus' the operator is fiercely protective of this maligned vehicle which carries an appropriate livery having been new to Black & White of Cheltenham. *Graham Ashworth*

The Knotty fleet provides an opportunity to ride on rare examples of buses from by-gone years especially AECs. Now restored to pristine condition, they can be found on services in the Potteries. *Top:* 17, JPA171K, new to London Country as RP71 is a Park Royal bodied Reliance and is seen on the Norton Estate while working through to Hanley. *Centre:* OFR983M is a dual-doored AEC Swift, one of many new to Blackpool where they were once the mainstay of the single-deck fleet. It is seen during 1993 in Burslem and carries lettering to celebrate the fifth anniversary of Knotty operations. *Bottom:* 23, JPF103K, is another AEC Swift but with Alexander bodywork that contrasts with the Marshall-bodied vehicle above. It is one of only three of the type believed to have survived and has been run by several operators, the last, appropriately, being Blue Triangle of Bootle. *Cliff Beeton*

LEONS

Leon's Coach Travel (Stafford) Ltd, Redhill Garage, First Avenue, Stafford,
Staffordshire, ST16 0RY

25	G805FJX	Scania K93CRB	Van Hool Alizée	C51FT	1990	Ex PMT, 1994
27	VRF566X	Mercedes-Benz L207D	Whittaker	M12	1982	
34	B192PFA	Mercedes-Benz L608D	PMT	C21F	1985	
35	LOI1454	Volvo B10M-61	Plaxton Viewmaster IV	C57F	1981	Ex Price, Halesowen, 1985
39	LOI9772	Volvo B10M-61	Van Hool Alizée	C49FT	1984	Ex Parks, Hamilton, 1986
40	8636PL	Scania K112CRB	Plaxton Paramount 3500 III	C49FT	1987	Ex PMT, 1994
41	9346PL	Scania K112CRB	Plaxton Paramount 3500 III	C49FT	1987	Ex PMT, 1994
43	A21FVT	Mercedes-Benz L508D	Reeve Burgess	C18F	1983	Ex Midland Red North, 1987
46	LOI7191	Volvo B10M-61	Van Hool Alizée	C49FT	1983	Ex Antler, Rugeley, 1987
48	E950LEH	Mercedes-Benz 811D	Optare StarRider	C29F	1988	
50	F150SRF	Volvo B10M-61	Van Hool Alizée	C53FT	1989	
51	RHP24W	Volvo B58-61	Plaxton Viewmaster IV	C57F	1980	Ex Wickson, Clayhanger, 1989
54	G360XEH	Scania K113CRB	Plaxton Paramount 3500 III	C49FT	1989	
55	G448BVT	Volvo B10M-61	Ikarus Blue Danube	C43FT	1990	
59	G655GFA	Scania K93CRB	Duple 320	C55F	1990	

Leons of Stafford is a company with a relatively short history, having been founded in 1971 by Mr
Leon Douglas. It has expanded rapidly in recent years and in January 1994 took over the Paramount
Leisure business and much of the coach fleet from PMT. Some vehicles acquired were due for early
disposal as this Handbook was prepared. New in 1989 was 48, E950LEH, a Mercedes-Benz 811D
coach with Optare StarRider bodywork. It is seen in the Granada Studio car park in Machester.
Graham Ashworth

60	H330JVT	Volvo B10M-60	Plaxton Paramount 3500 III	C51FT	1990	
64	E275HRY	Volvo B10M-61	Van Hool Alizée	C50FT	1988	Ex Sunspan, Birkenhead, 1991
65	LJI8160	Volvo B10M-61	Plaxton Paramount 3500 III	C49FT	1988	Ex Wallace Arnold, 1991
66	OIA1652	Volvo B58-61	Plaxton Supreme III	C53F	1978	Ex Gordon, Rotherham, 1991
68	J65SRE	Ford Transit VE6	Deansgate	M14	1992	
69	B258AGL	MCW Metroliner DR130/3	MCW	CH53/24FT	1984	Ex Western National, 1992
70	J62SRE	Volvo B10M-60	Plaxton Paramount 3500 III	C49FT	1992	
71	E752XHL	Mercedes-Benz 609D	Whittaker Europa	C24F	1988	Ex Wickson, Clayhanger, 1992
72	J413BPU	Ford Transit VE6	Ford	M14	1992	
73	K680BRE	Scania K113CRB	Plaxton Paramount 3500 III	C49FT	1993	
74	5888EH	Volvo B10M-61	Plaxton Paramount 3500	C49FT	1983	Ex Bushell, Burton, 1993
75	L2LCT	Volvo B10M-60	Jonckheere Deauville P599	C51FT	1993	
76	G117OGA	Mercedes-Benz 811D	Optare StarRider	C29F	1990	Ex Broomfield, Hawick, 1994
77	5702PL	Scania K92CRB	Van Hool Alizée	C55F	1989	Ex PMT, 1994
78	G806FJX	Scania K93CRB	Van Hool Alizée	C51FT	1990	Ex PMT, 1994
79	4327PL	Scania K112CRB	Plaxton Paramount 3500 III	C49FT	1987	Ex PMT, 1994
80	2335PL	Scania K112CRB	Van Hool Alizée	C51FT	1988	Ex PMT, 1994

Previous Registrations:

2335PL	E516YWF	LJI8160	E907UNW
4327PL	E39JRF	LOI1454	DUY596W
5702PL	F115UEH	LOI7191	STT605X
5888EH	FDH294Y, 1398NT, XUJ435Y	LOI9772	A644UGD
8636PL	E40JRF	OIA1652	EGD206T
9346PL	D226STM		

Livery: Cream and red.

Leons 59, G655EFA, a rear-engined Scania K93 with Duple 320 bodywork and was photographed while on an excursion to Betws-y-Coed. Purchased in 1990, it is one of several Scania products, but the only example with Duple coachwork. *Graham Ashworth*

LOFTY'S

Lofty's Tours Ltd, Morley Bridge, Bridge Trafford, Chester, Cheshire, CH2 4JR

Reg	Chassis	Body	Type	Year	Notes
ALG163J	Leyland Leopard PSU4B/4R	Plaxton Elite III	C45F	1971	Ex Hollis Coaches, Sealand, 1993
TGM201J	Daimler Fleetline CRG6LXB	Eastern Coach Works	H43/34F	1971	Ex Hollis Coaches, Sealand, 1993
UOD673R	Leyland Leopard PSU3E/4RT	Plaxton Supreme III	C47F	1977	Ex Grey Cars, Torquay, 1993
NSJ8R	Seddon Pennine 7	Alexander AYS	B53F	1976	Ex Western Scottish, 1987
SNU853R	Bristol LH6L	Eastern Coach Works	DP37F	1977	Ex Bluebird, 1993
WVO854S	Bristol LH6L	Eastern Coach Works	DP37F	1977	Ex Bluebird, 1993
WVO856S	Bristol LH6L	Eastern Coach Works	DP37F	1977	Ex Bluebird, 1993
KIW4390	Volvo B10M-61	Jonckheere Jubilee P50	C49FT	1984	Ex Cedric, Wivenhoe, 1993
D51RLG	Mercedes-Benz L608D	PMT Hanbridge	B20F	1986	
E569UHS	Volvo B10M-61	Plaxton Paramount 3500 III	C49FT	1987	Ex Parks, Hamilton, 1990
G958TCA	CVE Omni	CVE	B12FL	1990	
G959TCA	CVE Omni	CVE	B12FL	1990	
G960TCA	CVE Omni	CVE	B12FL	1990	
G27XBK	Iveco Daily 49.10	Phoenix	B25F	1990	
H611CGG	Mercedes-Benz 709D	Dormobile Routemaker	B29F	1991	
H612CGG	Mercedes-Benz 709D	Dormobile Routemaker	B29F	1991	
H613CGG	Mercedes-Benz 709D	Dormobile Routemaker	B29F	1991	
H183CNS	Mercedes-Benz 609D	Made-to-Measure	B26F	1991	
H184CNS	Mercedes-Benz 609D	Made-to-Measure	B26F	1991	
H185CNS	Mercedes-Benz 609D	Made-to-Measure	B26F	1991	
K731AOG	Peugeot-Talbot Pullman	Talbot	B18F	1993	
K732AOG	Peugeot-Talbot Pullman	Talbot	B18F	1993	
K106RNS	Mercedes-Benz 709D	Dormobile Routemaker	B29F	1993	

Previous Registrations:

ALG163J	NCK108J, 102UTF	KIW4390	A126XNH	
			UOD673R	SFJ145R, 4331PO

Livery: Turquoise and cream
Dial-a-Ride: G958-60TCA.

The mainstay of the minibus fleet operated by Loftys is the Mercedes-Benz with a total of seven operated currently. *Opposite, top,* is H185CNS, a 609D variant with Made-to-Measure bodywork, while *opposite, below* is H912XGA, a 709D with bodywork from Dormobile. Interestingly, these represent two recent victims of intense competition in the mini/midibus coachbuildling sector, FSV Dormobile having gone the way of Made-to-Measure in January 1994 *Richard Eversden*

One of two tri-axle Talbot Pullmans in the Lofty fleet, K732AOG is used on the Cheshire Bus services provided by this operator. On this occasion it is seen in Heswall, on the Wirral peninsular.
Graham Ashworth

LONGMYND

T G Evans, Britannia Bank Garage, Pontesbury, Shropshire, SY5 0QG

JRB914N	Bedford YRQ	Plaxton Elite III	C45F	1975	Ex O'Brien, Farnworth, 1980
BTU565S	Bedford YLQ	Plaxton Supreme III	C45F	1978	Ex Hanmers, Wrexham, 1980
NVR907W	Volvo B58-61	Plaxton Supreme IV	C57F	1980	Ex TRJ, Golbourne, 1984
LRC21W	Volvo B58-56	Plaxton Supreme IV	C53F	1980	Ex Luxicoaches, Borrowash, 1985
UAB943Y	Volvo B10M-61	Jonckheere Jubilee P90	C53FT	1983	Ex DRM, Bromyard, 1990
TGE93	Volvo B10M-61	Jonckheere Jubilee P90	C51FT	1984	Ex West Kingsdown Coaches, 1986
C377MAW	Volvo B10M-61	Plaxton Paramount 3500 II	C49FT	1986	
E504KNV	Volvo B10M-61	Jonckheere Jubilee P599	C57F	1988	Ex Tellings-Golden Miller, 1991
E170OMD	Volvo B10M-61	Plaxton Paramount 3200 III	C57F	1988	Ex Frames Rickards, Brentford, 1993
E311OMG	Volvo B10M-61	Plaxton Paramount 3200 III	C53F	1988	
F584BAW	Volvo B10M-61	Jonckheere Jubilee P599	C51FT	1988	
F969HGE	Volvo B10M-61	Plaxton Paramount 3200 III	C57F	1989	Ex Parks, Hamilton, 1990
F210PNR	Toyota Coaster HB31R	Caetano Optimo	C21F	1989	Ex Horseshoe, London N15, 1991
G30POD	Volkswagen Transporter	Devon Conversions	M11	1989	
G839GNV	Volvo B10M-60	Jonckheere Deauville P599	C51FT	1990	Ex Roffey, Flimwell, 1991
K1TGE	Volvo B10M-60	Jonckheere Deauville P599	C51FT	1993	
L2TGE	Mercedes-Benz 811D	Plaxton Beaver	DP33F	1993	

Previous Registrations:

EJX355V	LUA241V, 496WNN	UAB943Y	NVV552Y, MOI3565
TGE93	A118CNH	UMB945V	CEB139V, RCM632

Livery: White, red and black.

Although primarily an operator of tours and excursions, Longmynd Coaches has a large number of school contract services in the Shrewsbury area. C377MAW, in common with the majority of the coaches in the fleet, is a Volvo B10M. The 53-seat bodywork is by Plaxton to its Paramount 3200 Mark II design, the shortest-lived for the three phases of production.
Graham Ashworth

MERCURY

A J Degnan, Whitchurch Road, Spurstow, Cheshire, CW6 9TD

MJP516W	Volkswagen LT28	Devon Conversions	M12	1981	Ex Leece, Spurstow, 1984
D920MVU	Mercedes-Benz 609D	Made-to-Measure	B18FL	1986	Ex Walsh, Middleton, 1989
D81BCK	Freight Rover Sherpa	Elme	C16F	1987	Ex Brooklyn, London SW13, 1991
D29PVS	Freight Rover Sherpa	Dormobile	B16F	1987	Ex Inverness Traction, 1990
D223GLJ	Freight Rover Sherpa	Dormobile	B16F	1987	Ex Happy Days, Woodseaves, 1992
F388CKU	Mercedes-Benz 609D	Whittaker Europa	C24F	1988	Ex Belmont Ambassador, 1992
G771FJC	Volkswagen LT55	Optare City Pacer	DP25F	1989	Ex KMP, Llanberis, 1993
G774FJC	Volkswagen LT55	Optare City Pacer	DP25F	1989	Ex KMP, Llanberis, 1993
G214AHP	Peugeot-Talbot Pullman	Talbot	B22F	1990	Ex Transcity, Sidcup, 1993

Livery: White and blue

Two of the Volkswagen LT55s with Optare City Pacer bodywork used on the Dinorwic power station service previously operated by KMP have been added to the Mercury minibus operation based on the Cheshire village of Spurstow. G771FJC is seen at Ravensmoor on the service to Wrenbury, which continues back to Nantwich through Whitchurch and Audlem. *Graham Ashworth*

Several Cheshire Bus services and school contracts in north Shropshire and south Cheshire are provided by Merediths of Malpas, a village to the east of the A41 Chester to Whitchurch road. Several interesting vehicles are retained, one of which is VRR862G, a Bedford SB5 with Plaxton Panorama I style bodywork. *Graham Ashworth*

Until very recently, the double-deck requirement was met by a former London Transport DMS, OJD175R, with MCW bodywork. This vehicle has now been replaced, but was photographed to show the adaptions made to the livery to cater for school contract work. *Graham Ashworth*

MEREDITH

Meredith Coaches, Lydgate, Well Street, Malpas, Cheshire, SY14 8DE

GUJ356	Bedford OB	Duple Vista	C29F	1950	Ex Mid Wales, Newtown, 1976
VRR862G	Bedford SB5	Plaxton Panorama 1	C41F	1969	Ex Eardington Tours, 1980
OFC902H	Bristol VRT/SL6G	Eastern Coach Works	H39/31F	1970	Ex South Midland, 1987
SCS363M	Leyland Leopard PSU3/3R	Alexander AY	DP53F	1974	Ex Strathtay Scottish, 1987
SCS365M	Leyland Leopard PSU3/3R	Alexander AY	DP53F	1974	Ex Strathtay Scottish, 1987
852RKN	Leyland Leopard PSU3E/4R	Plaxton Supreme III Express	C53F	1978	Ex Roberts, Aberystwyth, 1989
798MMA	Ford R1114	Plaxton Supreme III	C53F	1978	
510UMA	Ford R1114	Plaxton Supreme III	C53F	1978	
USO187S	Ford R1114	Alexander AYS	B53F	1978	Ex Strathtay Scottish, 1987
RLS468T	Ford R1014	Alexander AYS	B45F	1979	Ex Strathtay Scottish, 1987
469KNP	Leyland Leopard PSU5C/4R	Plaxton Supreme IV	C53F	1979	Ex Copeland, Meir, 1992
NAX511	Leyland Leopard PSU3F/5R	Plaxton Supreme IV Express	C53F	1980	Ex Evans, Manmoel, 1992
YUO44W	Ford R1114	Plaxton Supreme IV	C53F	1980	Ex Bennett, Gloucester, 1994
JED904	Ford R1114	Plaxton Supreme IV	C53F	1981	
884MMB	Volvo B10M-61	Plaxton Paramount 3200	C53F	1983	
122BLM	Volvo B10M-61	Plaxton Paramount 3200 II	C53F	1985	
E135RAX	Freight Rover Sherpa	Carlyle Citybus 2	B20F	1987	Ex Phil Anslow, Garndiffaith, 1993
OLG7	Volvo B10M-61	Plaxton Paramount 3500 III	C49FT	1988	
JCM396	Volvo B10M-60	Plaxton Paramount 3200 III	C53F	1989	
684DYX	Volvo B10M-60	Plaxton Paramount 3200 III	C53F	1989	Ex Applebys, Conisholme, 1993
KSV408	Volvo B10M-61	Plaxton Paramount 3200 III	C57F	1989	Ex Alexander's, Aberdeen, 1992
WAW367	Volvo B10M-60	Plaxton Paramount 3200 III	C53F	1989	Ex Wallace Arnold, 1992

Previous Registrations:

122BLM	From new	JCM396	F238OFP
469KNP	EDF270T, MIB614, ARF930T	JED904	WCA893W
510UMA	EDM888S	KSV408	F102HSO
684DYX	F511NFW, KRO718, F521RTL	NAX511	CEP117V
798MMA	ATU887S, 2801DK, ETU841S	OLG7	E400BTU
852RKN	VAV986S	WAW367	F432DUG
884MMB	From new		

Livery: Beige, yellow and red

Featured recently in the Corgi model of the Bedford OB is GUJ356, an example of the OB purchased by the Meredith family from Mid Wales Motorways in 1976. It can often be seen promoting the business at local events.
Graham Ashworth

Midland now has 16 Dodge S46s with Northern Counties bodywork in service. These have been acquired from sister companies C-Line and Bee Line. No.367, D434NNA, photographed in Stafford was acquired from the former in 1993. *Colin Lloyd*

Passing through Park Road, Cannock, on local service 26 is Midland's 218, H708LOL, one of five Freight Rover Sherpas added to the fleet commencing in the Autumn of 1990. *Keith Grimes*

MIDLAND

Midland Red (North) Ltd, Delta Way, Longford Road, Cannock,
Staffordshire, WS11 3XB

Depots: Delta Way, Cannock; Bus Station, Crewe; Bus Station, Macclesfield, Oswald Road, Oswestry, Ditherington, Shrewsbury, Silkmore Lane, Stafford; Aldergate, Tamworth; Charlton Street, Wellington. Outstations are at Abermule, Bridgnorth, Congleton, Etruria and Woodseaves.

| 1 | TR6147 | Bristol LH6L | Hants & Dorset(1982) | Ch25F | 1974 | Ex Shamrock & Rambler, 1988 |

MERCEDES BENZ 811D 1994 MARSHALL B31F

451 M451EDH
452 M452EDH
453 M453EDH
454 M454EDH
455 M455EDH
456 M456EDH
457 M457 EDH
458 M458EDH
459 M459 EDH
460 M460 EDH
461 M461 EDH
462 M462 EDH

82-110		Ford Transit VE6		Dormobile		B16F		1986-87			
82	D82CFA	90	D90CFA	95	D95CFA	101	D101CFA	105	D105CFA
84	D84CFA	91	D91CFA	96	D96CFA	102	D102CFA	107	D107CFA
86	D86CFA	92	D92CFA	97	D97CFA	103	D103CFA	109	D109CFA
88	D88CFA	93	D93CFA	98	D98CFA	104	D104CFA	110	D110CFA

Several of Midland's depots used marketing names and differing liveries during the 1980s in order to show local identity. The use of the Midland name and livery was revived during 1989 and now a traditional, corporate identity has returned. Once in the blue and yellow livery of Hotspur was 21, C321URF, a Ford Transit with Dormobile bodywork.
Keith Grimes

112-118 — Ford Transit 190D — Carlyle B16F — 1986 — Ex Shamrock & Rambler, 1988

112	D202FFX	113	D203FFX	115	D205FFX	116	D206FFX	118	D208FFX

127	B409NJF	Ford Transit 190D	Rootes	B16F	1985	Ex Midland Fox, 1989
180	F39HOD	Ford Transit VE6	Dormobile	B20F	1988	Ex Panda Hire, Exeter, 1990

181-191 — Ford Transit VE6 — Dormobile — B18F — 1991

181	H181DHA	183	H183DHA	185	H185DHA	187	H187EHA	189	H189EHA
182	H182DHA	184	H184DHA	186	H186EHA	188	H188EHA	191	H191EHA

202	F452XON	Freight Rover Sherpa	Carlyle Citybus 2	B20F	1988	Ex Freight Rover demonstrator, 1988
212	F44XVP	Iveco Daily 40.6	Carlyle Dailybus 2	B21F	1989	Ex Carlyle demonstrator, 1989

218-229 — Freight Rover Sherpa — Carlyle Citybus 2 — B20F — 1990-91

218	H708LOL	219	H709LOL	220	H710LOL	221	H731LOL	229	H729LOL

230-234 — Freight Rover Sherpa — Carlyle Citybus 2 — B20F — 1987 — 230-3 ex London & Country, 1990 / 234 ex Shamrock & Rambler, 1989

230	E230NFX	231	E231NFX	232	E232NFX	233	E233NFX	234	E234NFX

255	D115NON	Freight Rover Sherpa	Carlyle	B20F	1987	Ex Bee Line Buzz, 1991
259	D219OOJ	Freight Rover Sherpa	Carlyle	B20F	1987	Ex King Offa Travel, Westbury, 1992
260	D230OOJ	Freight Rover Sherpa	Carlyle	B20F	1987	Ex King Offa Travel, Westbury, 1992
275	F275CEY	Iveco Daily 49.10	Robin Hood City Nippy	B21F	1988	Ex Crosville Wales, 1991
283	F483EJC	Iveco Daily 49.10	Carlyle Dailybus	DP25F	1989	Ex Crosville Wales, 1991
284	F484EJC	Iveco Daily 49.10	Carlyle Dailybus	DP25F	1989	Ex Crosville Wales, 1991
285	F485EJC	Iveco Daily 49.10	Carlyle Dailybus	DP25F	1989	Ex Crosville Wales, 1991
286	F486EJC	Iveco Daily 49.10	Carlyle Dailybus	DP25F	1989	Ex Crosville Wales, 1991
296	F276CEY	Iveco Daily 49.10	Robin Hood City Nippy	DP25F	1988	Ex Crosville Wales, 1991

Opposite top: **Photographed passing the William Salt Library in Stafford is Midland 1723, B103KPF. This Leyland Tiger is one of a several acquired from London & Country in 1991. Prior to its entry into service it was rebodied by East Lancashire as a 61-seat bus. It is taking up service on route 432 which serves a rural area in West Staffordshire previously covered by Happy Days.** *Colin Lloyd*

Opposite bottom: **Midland 2010, G510SFT, is a Leyland Olympian with Northern Counties bodywork, here leaving Aldergate in Tamworth. The vehicle was originally with Kentish Bus, prior to Bee Line Buzz in Manchester, from where it came to Midland.** *Colin Lloyd*

Operating one of Cannock's local services is Midland's 231, E231NFX. One Freight Rover Sherpa was taken from the Shamrock & Rambler fleet in 1989 and this was joined by four others in 1990 after a period with London & Country, where this example was numbered SL2. *Keith Grimes*

301-328   Iveco Daily 49-10S   Carlyle Dailybus   B23F   1989-90

301	F601EHA	307	F607EHA	312	F612EHA	318	F618EHA	324	F624EHA
302	F602EHA	308	F608EHA	313	F613EHA	319	F619EHA	325	F625EHA
303	F603EHA	309	F609EHA	314	F614EHA	320	F620EHA	326	F626EHA
304	F604EHA	310	F610EHA	315	F615EHA	322	F622EHA	327	G327PHA
305	F605EHA	311	F611EHA	316	F616EHA	323	F623EHA	328	G328PHA
306	F606EHA								

329-339   Renault-Dodge S56   Northern Counties   B23F   1990-91

329	H329DHA	332	H332DHA	334	H334DHA	336	H336DHA	338	H338DHA
330	H330DHA	333	H433DHA	335	H335DHA	337	H337DHA	339	H339DHA
331	H331DHA								

340-350   Renault-Dodge S56   Northern Counties   B23F   1988   Ex North Western, 1991

340	E90WCM	343	E93WCM	345	E95WCM	347	E97WCM	349	E99WCM
341	E91WCM	344	E94WCM	346	E96WCM	348	E98WCM	350	E611LFV

351	D401NNA	Renault-Dodge S46	Northern Counties	B22F	1987	Ex Bee Line Buzz, 1992
352	D402NNA	Renault-Dodge S46	Northern Counties	B22F	1987	Ex Bee Line Buzz, 1992
353	D448NNA	Renault-Dodge S46	Northern Counties	D22F	1987	Ex Bee Line Buzz, 1992
354	D432NNA	Renault-Dodge S46	Northern Counties	B22F	1987	Ex Bee Line Buzz, 1992
355	D420NNA	Renault-Dodge S46	Northern Counties	B22F	1987	Ex C-Line, 1992
356	D436NNA	Renault-Dodge S46	Northern Counties	B22F	1987	Ex C-Line, 1992
357	D430NNA	Renault-Dodge S46	Northern Counties	B22F	1987	Ex Bee Line Buzz, 1993
358	D438NNA	Renault-Dodge S46	Northern Counties	B22F	1987	Ex Bee Line Buzz, 1993
359	D319DEF	Renault-Dodge S56	Northern Counties	B22F	1988	Ex Cleveland Transit, 1992
360	E110JPL	Renault-Dodge S46	Northern Counties	B23F	1987	Ex C-Line, 1992
361	D422NNA	Renault-Dodge S46	Northern Counties	B22F	1987	Ex Bee Line Buzz, 1992
362	D322DEF	Renault-Dodge S56	Northern Counties	B22F	1988	Ex Cleveland Transit, 1992
363	D450NNA	Renault-Dodge S46	Northern Counties	B22F	1987	Ex Bee Line Buzz, 1992
364	D423NNA	Renault-Dodge S46	Northern Counties	B22F	1987	Ex Bee Line Buzz, 1992
365	E325JVN	Renault-Dodge S56	Northern Counties	B22F	1988	Ex Cleveland Transit, 1992
366	D429NNA	Renault-Dodge S46	Northern Counties	B22F	1987	Ex Bee Line Buzz, 1993
367	D434NNA	Renault-Dodge S46	Northern Counties	B22F	1987	Ex Bee Line Buzz, 1993
368	D440NNA	Renault-Dodge S46	Northern Counties	B22F	1987	Ex Bee Line Buzz, 1993
369	D441NNA	Renault-Dodge S46	Northern Counties	B22F	1987	Ex Bee Line Buzz, 1993
370	D444NNA	Renault-Dodge S46	Northern Counties	B22F	1987	Ex Bee Line Buzz, 1993
400	G150GOL	Iveco Daily 49.10	Carlyle Dailybus 2	B25F	1990	Ex Carlyle, 1991

411-428   Mercedes-Benz 811D   Carlyle   B33F   1989-90   Ex C-Line, 1991-92
414 ex Bee Line Buzz, 1993

411	G111TND	415	G115TND	421	G121TJA	426	G126TJA	428	G128TJA
414	G114TND	417	G117TND	422	G122TJA	427	G127TJA		

431-436   Mercedes-Benz 811D   LHE   B31F   1990   Ex C-Line, 1992

431	H131CDB	433	H133CDB	434	H134CDB	435	H135CDB	436	H136CDB
432	H132CDB								

448	F148USX	Mercedes-Benz 811D	Alexander AM	DP33F	1988	Ex Happy Days, Woodseaves, 1991
480	JOX480P	Leyland National 11351/1R		B49F	1976	

482-486   Mercedes-Benz L608D   Reeve Burgess   DP19F   1986   Ex C-Line, 1992

482	D202SKD	483	D203SKD	484	D204SKD	485	D205SKD	486	D206SKD

490-495   Mercedes-Benz 709D   Reeve Burgess Beaver   B25F   1989   Ex C-Line, 1992

490	F700LCA	492	F702KMA	493	F703KFM	494	F704KFM	495	F705KFM
491	F701KMA								

497	C707JMB	Mercedes-Benz L608D	Reeve Burgess	B20F	1986	Ex C-Line, 1992
498	C708JMB	Mercedes-Benz L608D	Reeve Burgess	B20F	1986	Ex C-Line, 1992
499	JOX499P	Leyland National 11351/1R		B49F	1976	

1990 purchases of minibuses introduced Carlyle-bodied Iveco 49.10 models. No.328, G328PHA, was registered as part of a policy to obtain HA registrations when available. Since the closure of Dudley LVLO, it is unlikely that further, similar registrations will be obtainable. This vehicle is in the basic yellow and red livery applied to minibuses in 1990. *Bill Potter*

Many of the vehicles acquired with the C-Line operation have already been painted into the Midland livery. Displaying signs for both Cheshire Bus and Staffordshire Bus services is 411, G111TND, a Mercedes-Benz 811D with Caryle bodywork. It is seen departing Hanley bus station for Leighton hospital in February 1994. *Keith Grimes*

| 501 | H501GHA | Dennis Dart 8.5SDL3003 | | East Lancashire EL2000 | B35F | 1991 | | |

502-523
Dennis Dart 9SDL3034 — East Lancashire EL2000 — B33F — 1994

502	L502BNX	507	L507BNX	512	L512BNX	516	L516BNX	520	L620BNX
503	L503BNX	508	L508BNX	513	L513BNX	517	L517BNX	521	L521BNX
504	L504BNX	509	L509BNX	514	L514BNX	518	L618BNX	522	L522BNX
505	L605BNX	510	L510BNX	515	L515BNX	519	L519BNX	523	L523BNX
506	L506BNX	511	L511BNX						

530-600
Leyland National 11351A/1R — B49F — 1976-77 532/57 ex Midland Red East, 1982-83

530	JOX530P	537	NOE537R	557	NOE557R	575	NOE575R	600	NOE600R
532	JOX522P	538	NOE538R	574	NOE574R	599	NOE599R		

635-700
Leyland National 11351A/1R — B49F — 1977-78 639/47/8/52 ex Midland Red East, 1982-83

635	PUK635R	652	PUK652R	687	TOF687S	693	TOF693S	697	TOF697S
637	PUK637R	683	TOF683S	688	TOF688S	694	TOF694S	698	TOF698S
639	PUK639R	684	TOF684S	691	TOF691S	695	TOF695S	699	TOF699S
647	PUK647R	685	TOF685S	692	TOF692S	696	TOF696S	700	TOF700S
648	PUK648R								

| 701 | J701NHA | Dennis Dart 9.8SDL3004 | | East Lancashire EL2000 | B40F | 1991 | | |

Two Dennis Darts, one 9-metre and one to the shorter length of 8.5-metres were added to the fleet in 1991. The former was numbered 501, H501GHA, and has recently been followed by twenty-two further examples. Initially based in Crewe 501 has joined the others in Telford where they have, in the main, replaced minibuses. *Graham Ashworth*

The North Midlands Bus Handbook

Leyland National 901, TOF701S, was acquired from Midland Red in 1981. However this vehicle has been extensively modernised. The most obvious difference from its original condition is the removal of the roof pod to allow its operation on certain services in Stafford. There are seven similar 11-metre vehicles in the Midland fleet and to avoid confusion with their 'podded' stablemates are numbered in the 901-90 series. *Colin Lloyd*

Midland 575, NOE575R, shown here in Shrewsbury, is one of the few survivors of the vehicles taken over when Midland Red was split-up in September 1981. Leyland Nationals still dominate the Shrewsbury services which operate round the town centre on a one-way gyratory system. *Malc McDonald*

The latest delivery of twenty-two Dennis Darts is represented by 507, L507BNX, seen working service 3 returning to Wellington from Telford shopping centre. This batch was the first to be delivered in the new livery and with the new fleetname. *Bill Potter*

Four Leyland Tigers from the Timeline operation were added to the Midland fleet in 1993. New to Shearings, they have the Alexander N-type body and were assembled at the Belfast plant. Departing from its base in Tamworth on a cold winters day is 1745, E25UNE.
Bill Potter

Working a Staffordshire sponsored Sunday contract, Leyland Tiger Plaxton coach 1698 is seen in Shelton, not far from the centre of Stoke on Trent. Route 53 operates between Keele and Baddeley Green. Now numbered 1698, A898KAH, was acquired by Midland from C-Line with that operation.
Cliff Beeton

702-767

	Leyland National 11351A/1R			B49F		1977-80			
702	TOF702S	**705**	TOF705S	**719**	TOF719S	**764**	BVP764V	**766**	BVP766V
703	TOF703S	**717**	TOF717S	**763**	BVP763V	**765**	BVP765V	**767**	BVP767V
704	TOF704S	**718**	TOF718S						

796	UHG758R	Leyland National 11351A/1R	B49F	1977	Ex North Western, 1989
825	NTC625M	Leyland National 1151/1R/0401	B49F	1973	Ex C-Line, 1992
859	TPE159S	Leyland National 11351A/1R	B49F	1978	Ex Alder Valley, 1990
863	TPE163S	Leyland National 11351A/1R	B49F	1978	Ex Alder Valley, 1990
866	TPE166S	Leyland National 11351A/1R	B49F	1978	Ex Alder Valley, 1990
872	GMB372T	Leyland National 11351A/1R	B49F	1979	Ex C-Line, 1992
873	GMB373T	Leyland National 11351A/1R	B49F	1979	Ex Crosville, 1989
874	GMB374T	Leyland National 11351A/1R	B49F	1979	Ex Bee Line Buzz, 1990
875	LFR875X	Leyland National 2 NL106AL11/1R East Lancs Greenway (1992) B41F		1982	Ex C-Line, 1992
876	GMB376T	Leyland National 11351A/1R	B49F	1979	Ex Crosville, 1989
878	GMB378T	Leyland National 11351A/1R	B49F	1979	Ex Crosville, 1989
883	GMB383T	Leyland National 11351A/1R	B49F	1979	Ex C-Line, 1992
890	GMB390T	Leyland National 11351A/1R	B49F	1979	Ex Crosville, 1989
891	KMA401T	Leyland National 11351A/1R	B49F	1979	Ex C-Line, 1992
892	KMA402T	Leyland National 11351A/1R	B49F	1979	Ex C-Line, 1992
895	BPL495T	Leyland National 10351B/1R	B41F	1979	Ex London & Country, 1988

901-990

	Leyland National 11351A/1R			B49F*		1976-80 953 ex Midland Red East, 1982 *953 is B45F, 968 is B41F			
901	TOF701S	**953**	PUK653R	**968**	BVP768V	**969**	BVP969V	**990**	TOF690S
917	JOX517P								

1041-1096

	Leyland National 10351B/1R			B44F		1978-79 Ex Crosville Wales, 1991 1056/67 ex C-Line, 1992			
1041	EMB641S	**1056**	GMB666T	**1066**	HMA566T	**1079**	ODM679V	**1095**	JTU595T
1042	EMB642S	**1059**	HMA559T	**1067**	GMB667T	**1080**	JTU580T	**1096**	JTU596T
1052	GMB652T	**1062**	GMB662T	**1070**	HMA570T	**1087**	JTU587T		

1201-1210

Dennis Falcon HC SDA421   East Lancashire EL2000   B48F   1990   Ex London & Country, 1991

1201	G301DPA	**1207**	G307DPA	**1208**	G308DPA	**1209**	G309DPA	**1210**	G310DPA
1206	G306DPA								

1211-1219

Dennis Falcon HC SDA423   East Lancashire EL2000   B48F   1992

1211	K211UHA	**1213**	K213UHA	**1215**	K215UHA	**1217**	K217UHA	**1219**	K219UHA
1212	K212UHA	**1214**	K214UHA	**1216**	K216UHA	**1218**	K218UHA		

1301	JMB328T	Leyland Leopard PSU3E/4R	Duple Dominant II Express	C49F	1978	Ex Crosville, 1989
1423	GOE136V	Leyland Leopard PSU3E/4R	Plaxton Supreme IV Express	C53F	1979	Ex Shamrock & Rambler, 1988
1516	B516OEH	Leyland Tiger TRCTL11/3RH	Duple Laser 2	C53F	1984	
1522	BPR102Y	Leyland Tiger TRCTL11/3R	Duple Laser	C50F	1983	Ex London & Country, 1991
1526	BPR106Y	Leyland Tiger TRCTL11/3R	Duple Laser	C50F	1983	Ex London & Country, 1991
1527	BPR107Y	Leyland Tiger TRCTL11/3R	Duple Laser	C50F	1983	Ex London & Country, 1991
1604	B604OEH	Leyland Tiger TRCTL11/3RH	Duple Laser 2	C55F	1984	
1605	B605OEH	Leyland Tiger TRCTL11/3RH	Duple Laser 2	C55F	1984	
1606	B606OEH	Leyland Tiger TRCTL11/3RH	Duple Laser 2	C55F	1984	
1607	B607OEH	Leyland Tiger TRCTL11/3RH	Duple Laser 2	C55F	1984	
1615	A215PEV	Leyland Tiger TRCTL11/2R	Duple Dominant IV Express	C53F	1983	Ex Southend, 1990
1618	A118EPA	Leyland Tiger TRCTL11/2R	Plaxton Paramount 3200	C53F	1983	Ex C-Line, 1992
1639	A139EPA	Leyland Tiger TRCTL11/2R	Plaxton Paramount 3200	C53F	1984	Ex C-Line, 1992
1642	D442CNR	Volvo B10M-61	Plaxton Paramount 3200 III	C46FT	1987	Ex Express Travel, Perth, 1994
1653	TDC853X	Leyland Tiger TRCTL11/2R	Duple Dominant IV Express	C53F	1982	Ex Shamrock & Rambler, 1988
1654	TDC854X	Leyland Tiger TRCTL11/2R	Duple Dominant IV Express	C53F	1982	Ex Shamrock & Rambler, 1988
1660	A160EPA	Leyland Tiger TRCTL11/3R	Plaxton Paramount 3200	C50FT	1984	Ex C-Line, 1992
1698	A898KAH	Leyland Tiger TRCTL11/3R	Plaxton Paramount 3200	C53F	1983	Ex C-Line, 1992

1701-1709

Leyland Tiger TRCTL11/2R   Duple Dominant   B51F   1984

1701	A701HVT	**1703**	A703HVT	**1705**	A705HVT	**1707**	A707HVT	**1709**	A709HVT
1702	A702HVT	**1704**	A704HVT	**1706**	A706HVT	**1708**	A708HVT		

1710-1720

Leyland Tiger TRCTL11/2R   East Lancashire (1989)   B51F*   1982   Ex London & Country, 1989
*1710/3/4/8 are DP49F, 1712 is B55F.

1710	TPC101X	**1713**	TPC103X	**1715**	WPH125Y	**1717**	TPC107X	**1719**	WPH139Y
1711	WPH121Y	**1714**	TPC104X	**1716**	WPH126Y	**1718**	TPC114X	**1720**	WPH122Y
1712	TPC102X								

1721-1730

Leyland Tiger TRCTL11/3RH   East Lancashire (1991)   B61F   1983-86   1721-9 ex London & Country, 1991
1730 ex County, 1991

1721	C141SPB	**1723**	B103KPF	**1725**	B105KPF	**1728**	B108KPF	**1730**	YPJ207Y
1722	B102KPF	**1724**	B104KPF	**1726**	C262SPC	**1729**	B109KPF		

1733	LTS93X	Leyland Tiger TRCTL11/3R	East Lancashire (1992)	B61F	1982	Ex Tame Valley, Birmingham, 1992
1735	DJN25X	Leyland Tiger TRCTL11/2R	East Lancashire (1992)	B55F	1982	Ex County, 1992
1737	UJN430Y	Leyland Tiger TRCTL11/2R	East Lancashire (1991)	B55F	1982	Ex County, 1991
1738	WPH118Y	Leyland Tiger TRCTL11/2R	East Lancashire (1992)	B55F	1983	Ex County, 1991
1740	AAX590A	Leyland Tiger TRCTL11/3R	East Lancashire (1993)	B61F	1983	Ex Rhondda, 1992
1742	A42SMA	Leyland Tiger TRCTL11/2R	East Lancashire (1992)	B55F	1984	Ex North Western, 1991
1743	WPH123Y	Leyland Tiger TRCTL11/2R	East Lancashire (1992)	B55F	1983	Ex County, 1991
1745	E25UNE	Leyland Tiger TRBTL11/3ARZA	Alexander N	B53F	1988	Ex Timeline, Leigh, 1993
1746	E26UNE	Leyland Tiger TRBTL11/3ARZA	Alexander N	B53F	1988	Ex Timeline, Leigh, 1993
1747	E27UNE	Leyland Tiger TRBTL11/3ARZA	Alexander N	B53F	1988	Ex Timeline, Leigh, 1993
1748	E28UNE	Leyland Tiger TRBTL11/3ARZA	Alexander N	B53F	1988	Ex Timeline, Leigh, 1993

1801-1806

Dennis Dominator DDA1032   East Lancashire   H47/29F   1990

1801	G801THA	**1803**	H803AHA	**1804**	H804AHA	**1805**	H805AHA	**1806**	H806AHA
1802	G802THA								

1815-1871

Bristol VRT/SL3/6LXB   Eastern Coach Works   H43/31F   1980-81   Ex Crosville Wales, 1991
1871 ex C-Line, 1992

1815	YMB515W	**1820**	BMA520W	**1858**	VCA458W	**1867**	WTU467W	**1871**	WTU471W
1819	YMB519W	**1823**	BMA523W	**1860**	VCA460W	**1870**	WTU470W		

Midland has many Leyland Tigers in the fleet. Most of these are secondhand acquisitions from companies in the British Bus group. However, nine, all fitted with Duple Dominant bus bodywork were purchased new in 1984. One of these, 1705, A705HVT, is seen about to leave Wellington for Wolverhampton. *Bill Potter*

The East Lancashire EL2000 bodies have two different roof lines. The examples on the re-built Leyland Tigers have a thin cantrail while the Dennis vehicles feature a cantrail of some six inches. Of the former type, 1718, TPC114X, is seen in the old livery while waiting time at Wolverhampton bus station. *Keith Grimes*

1878	WTU478W	Bristol VRT/SL3/6LXC	Eastern Coach Works	H43/31F	1981	Ex C-Line, 1992
1884	WTU484W	Bristol VRT/SL3/6LXC	Eastern Coach Works	H43/31F	1981	Ex C-Line, 1992
1885	WTU485W	Bristol VRT/SL3/6LXC	Eastern Coach Works	H43/31F	1981	Ex C-Line, 1992
1898	JMB398T	Bristol VRT/SL3/501	Eastern Coach Works	H43/31F	1979	Ex C-Line, 1992

1902-1910

		Leyland Olympian ONLXB/1R	Eastern Coach Works	H45/32F	1983	

1902	EEH902Y	**1904**	EEH904Y	**1906**	EEH906Y	**1909**	EEH909Y	**1910** EEH910Y
1903	EEH903Y	**1905**	EEH905Y	**1907**	EEH907Y			

1911	B911NBF	Leyland Olympian ONLXB/1R	Eastern Coach Works	DPH42/28F	1984	
1912	B912NBF	Leyland Olympian ONLXB/1R	Eastern Coach Works	DPH42/28F	1984	
1913	B913NBF	Leyland Olympian ONLXB/1R	Eastern Coach Works	DPH42/28F	1984	
1914	B197DTU	Leyland Olympian ONLXB/1R	Eastern Coach Works	H45/32F	1985	Ex Crosville, 1989
1915	B198DTU	Leyland Olympian ONLXB/1R	Eastern Coach Works	H45/32F	1985	Ex Crosville, 1989
1916	G916LHA	Leyland Olympian ON2R50G16ZA	East Lancashire	H45/29F	1989	
1917	G917LHA	Leyland Olympian ON2R50G16ZA	East Lancashire	H45/29F	1989	
1918	G918LHA	Leyland Olympian ON2R50G16ZA	East Lancashire	H45/29F	1989	
1919	G919LHA	Leyland Olympian ON2R50G16ZA	East Lancashire	H45/29F	1989	
1923	B203DTU	Leyland Olympian ONLXB/1R	Eastern Coach Works	DPH42/27F	1985	Ex Crosville Wales, 1990
1924	B204DTU	Leyland Olympian ONLXB/1R	Eastern Coach Works	DPH42/27F	1985	Ex Crosville Wales, 1990
1937	GFM107X	Leyland Olympian ONLXB/1R	Eastern Coach Works	H45/32F	1982	Ex Crosville, 1989
1938	PFM130Y	Leyland Olympian ONLXB/1R	Eastern Coach Works	H45/32F	1983	Ex Crosville, 1989
1950	A150UDM	Leyland Olympian ONLXB/1R	Eastern Coach Works	H45/32F	1983	Ex C-Line, 1992
1952	A152UDM	Leyland Olympian ONLXB/1R	Eastern Coach Works	H45/32F	1984	Ex C-Line, 1992
1954	A154UDM	Leyland Olympian ONLXB/1R	Eastern Coach Works	H45/32F	1984	Ex Crosville, 1989
1955	A155UDM	Leyland Olympian ONLXB/1R	Eastern Coach Works	H45/32F	1984	Ex Crosville, 1989
1972	A172VFM	Leyland Olympian ONLXB/1R	Eastern Coach Works	H45/32F	1984	Ex C-Line, 1992
2005	G505SFT	Leyland Olympian ONCL10/1RZ	Northern Counties Palatine	H47/30F	1989	Ex Bee Line Buzz, 1993
2007	G507SFT	Leyland Olympian ONCL10/1RZ	Northern Counties Palatine	H47/30F	1989	Ex Bee Line Buzz, 1993
2010	G510SFT	Leyland Olympian ONCL10/1RZ	Northern Counties Palatine	H47/30F	1989	Ex Bee Line Buzz, 1993
2011	G511SFT	Leyland Olympian ONCL10/1RZ	Northern Counties Palatine	H47/30F	1989	Ex Bee Line Buzz, 1993
2044	G644BPH	Volvo Citybus B10M-50	Northern Counties Palatine	H45/35F	1989	Ex Bee Line Buzz, 1993
2045	G645BPH	Volvo Citybus B10M-50	Northern Counties Palatine	H45/35F	1989	Ex Bee Line Buzz, 1993
2046	G646BPH	Volvo Citybus B10M-50	Northern Counties Palatine	H45/35F	1989	Ex Bee Line Buzz, 1993
2047	G647BPH	Volvo Citybus B10M-50	Northern Counties Palatine	H45/35F	1989	Ex Bee Line Buzz, 1993
2069	TPU69R	Leyland Atlantean AN68A/1R	Eastern Coach Works	H43/31F	1977	Ex C-Line, 1992

Named Vehicles:
1914 *Rear Admiral S L McArdle*, 1918 *Valour*, 1937 *Geoffrey Thompson*.

Previous Registrations:

AAX590A	A217VWO	LTS93X	VSS1X, WLT610
DJN25X	TPC106X, OIB3510	TR6147	NLJ516M
GOE136V	ELJ210V, 123TKM	UJN430Y	WPH124Y, FBZ2514

Livery: Red and gold

Most of the Leyland Olympians in the Midland fleet have Eastern Coach Works bodywork and date from the 1982-85 period. 1902, EEH902Y, is typical of these, and is one recently transferred to Macclesfield.
Cliff Beeton

Six Dennis Dominators were added to the fleet in 1990, and all were based at Crewe where they replaced Bristol VRTs. First of the batch, 1801, G801THA, shows off its East Lancashire bodywork as it manoeuvres in Hanley bus station. *Keith Grimes*

Midland's trunk routes between Birmingham and Tamworth - 110 through Sutton and 116 through Kingsbury - are now normally operated by eight vehicles purchased from Bee Line. Four of these vehicles, including 2046, G646BPH, are 80-seat Volvo B10M-50s with Northern Counties bodywork. The vehicle is seen unloading in Corporation Street, Tamworth. *Colin Lloyd*

MINSTERLEY MOTORS

Oakrim Ltd, Stiperstones, Minsterley, Shropshire, SY5 0LZ

510DMY	Leyland Leopard PSU3E/4R	Plaxton Elite III	C53F	1973	Ex Young, Romsley, 1987
RAX806M	Bedford YRT	Plaxton Elite Express III	C53F	1974	Ex Clun Valley Motors, 1989
ONL924M	Bedford YRT	Plaxton Elite III	C53F	1974	Ex Dore, Leafield, 1981
NWK10P	Bedford YLQ	Plaxton Supreme III	C45F	1976	Ex Nicholls, Broad Oak, 1991
MWB115P	Bedford YLQ	Plaxton Supreme III	C45F	1976	Ex Torr, Gedling, 1991
RRR520R	Bedford YMT	Plaxton Supreme III Express	C53F	1977	Ex Orion Travel, Hereford, 1989
PYG139R	Bedford YMT	Plaxton Supreme III	C53F	1977	Ex Yeomans, Hereford, 1989
SNM71R	Bedford YMT	Plaxton Supreme III	C53F	1977	Ex Delvo, Mytchett, 1990
CWA439T	Bedford YMT	Duple Dominant	B55F	1979	Ex Beeline, Warminster, 1993
MHP17V	Bedford YMT	Plaxton Supreme IV	C49F	1980	Ex Harry Shaw, Coventry, 1982
1877NT	Bedford YMT	Plaxton Supreme IV Express	C53F	1980	Ex Clun Valley Motors, 1991
JUS476Y	Mercedes-Benz L608D	Whittaker	C19F	1983	Ex Pasadena Roof Orchestra, 1990
9489PH	Bedford YNT	Plaxton Paramount 3500	C53F	1983	Ex Smith, Liss, 1991
A615KRT	Bedford YNT	Plaxton Paramount 3200	C53F	1984	Ex Ward, Alresford, 1990
G738VKK	Renault Master T35D	Jubilee	M16	1990	Ex Van, 1992

Previous Registrations:

1877NT	JRW787V	A615KRT	A253SBM, 866VNU
510DMY	KNR327L, 961CUF, FDH926L	9489PH	WJH503Y

Livery: Grey and blue

Still an uncommon type of minibus is the Renault Master. Minsterly Motors use their example on both commercial services and those operated on behalf of Shropshire Bus. G738VKK is seen about to leave Shrewsbury bus station in March 1994. The centre door has an electric sliding facility operated by the driver. *Bill Potter*

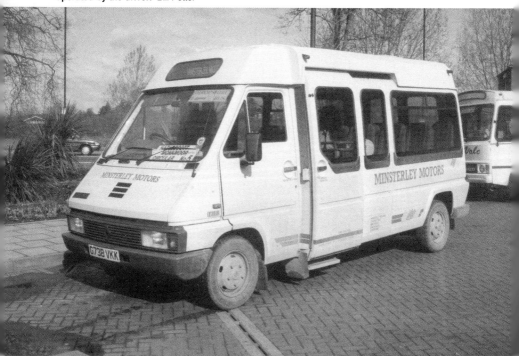

The North Midlands Bus Handbook

MOORLAND ROVER

G V Shaw, 107 Washerwall Lane, Werrington, Stoke-on-Trent,
Staffordshire, ST9 0LR

Depot: Weston Coyney

007	C549TJF	Ford Transit 190	Rootes	B16F	1986	Ex Stevensons, 1990
008	D823KWT	Freight Rover Sherpa	Dormobile	B16F	1987	Ex West Riding, 1991
009	D812KWT	Freight Rover Sherpa	Dormobile	B16F	1987	Ex West Riding, 1991
010	D770PTU	Freight Rover Sherpa	Dormobile	B16F	1987	Ex North Western, 1991
011	D757PTU	Freight Rover Sherpa	Dormobile	B16F	1987	Ex Bee Line Buzz, 1991
012	D217GLJ	Freight Rover Sherpa	Dormobile	B16F	1987	Ex North Western, 1991
013	D106UJC	Freight Rover Sherpa	Dormobile	B16F	1987	Ex Crosville Wales, 1991
014	D107UJC	Freight Rover Sherpa	Dormobile	B16F	1987	Ex Crosville Wales, 1991
015	D135NON	Freight Rover Sherpa	Carlyle	B18F	1987	Ex Bee Line Buzz, 1992
016	D587EWS	Freight Rover Sherpa	Dormobile	DP16F	1988	Ex Ribble, 1992
017	D746PTU	Freight Rover Sherpa	Dormobile	B16F	1988	Ex Thamesroute, London N5, 1992
018	D793RFM	Freight Rover Sherpa	Dormobile	B16F	1988	Ex Blue Bus, Horwich, 1992
019	D719PTU	Freight Rover Sherpa	Dormobile	B16F	1988	Ex Cooper, Ashton, 1993
020	D473CKV	Freight Rover Sherpa	Rootes	B18F	1988	Ex Dutton & Goldstraw, Bradnop, 1993
021	D466CKV	Freight Rover Sherpa	Rootes	B18F	1988	Ex Dutton & Goldstraw, Bradnop, 1993
022	C593TUT	Ford Transit 190	Dormobile	B16F	1988	Ex Stevensons, 1993
	D575EWS	Freight Rover Sherpa	Dormobile	B16F	1986	Ex Badgerline, 1993
	D587EWS	Freight Rover Sherpa	Dormobile	B16F	1986	Ex Badgerline, 1993

Livery: Blue and white

Moorland Rover operate a fleet of minibuses, most of which are Freight Rovers, from a base in Weston Coyney, near Stoke on Trent. One of a pair from Crosville Wales is 013, D106UJC, now painted in the fleet livery of blue and white. *Keith Grimes*

MORRIS

T Morris, 14 Meadowside, Loggerheads, Market Drayton, Shropshire, TF9 4RB

| NBF957V | Ford Transit 160 | Dormobile | M16 | 1980 | Ex Copelands, 1993 |

Previous Registrations:
NBF957V   55WEH

N C B

NC, DN & PR Brown, Edstaston Garage, Wem, Shropshire, SY4 5RF

MRY53P	Bedford YMT	Duple Dominant	C53F	1976	Ex Glennie, New Mill, 1989
PDK308S	Bedford YLQ	Duple Dominant	C45F	1977	Ex Garratt, Leicester, 1990
KDM760T	Bedford YMT	Duple Dominant II	C53F	1979	Ex Frazer, Rufford, 1985
A32GJT	Bedford YNT	Duple Laser	C53F	1984	Ex Marchwood, Totton, 1987
A33GJT	Bedford YNT	Duple Laser	C53F	1984	Ex Marchwood, Totton, 1987
B977HNT	Bedford YNV Venturer	Duple Laser 2	C55F	1985	
F374DUX	Volvo B10M-60	Duple 340	C55F	1988	
F971HGE	Volvo B10M-60	Plaxton Paramount 3500 III	C57F	1989	Ex Parks, Hamilton, 1990
J1NCB	Volvo B10M-60	Jonckheere Deauville P599	C51FT	1991	
K1NCB	Volvo B10M-60	Jonckheere Deauville P599	C55FT	1992	
L1NCB	Volvo B10M-60	Plaxton Premiére 350	C53FT	1994	

Livery: Cream and brown

NCB has purchased three new vehicles in as many years, managing to secure the appropriate 1NBC plates. The latest example, L1NCB carries a Plaxton Premiére body and should be in service by Easter. K1NCB is one of two with Jonckheere Deauville bodywork and is seen while taking a break at services on the M1 when heading for London. *Bill Potter*

OWENS

F G Owen, 36 Beatrice Street, Oswestry, Shropshire, SY11 1QG

E506JWP	Dennis Javelin 12SDA1908	Plaxton Paramount 3200 III	C49FT	1988	Ex Go-Whittle, 1992
E650JWP	Dennis Javelin 12SDA1908	Plaxton Paramount 3200 III	C49FT	1988	Ex Go-Whittle, 1992
G851VAY	Dennis Javelin 12SDA1907	Duple 320	C57F	1989	
G852VAY	Dennis Javelin 12SDA1907	Duple 320	C57F	1989	
G106AVX	Dennis Javelin 12SDA1912	Duple 320	C52FT	1990	Ex Colchester, 1993
H154OEP	Nissan Urvan	Deansgate	M8	1990	
H236RUX	Hestair Duple SDA1512	Duple 425	C51FT	1991	
H237RUX	Hestair Duple SDA1512	Duple 425	C51FT	1991	
K879EAW	Volvo B10M-60	Plaxton Première 350	C49FT	1993	
K106UFP	Toyota Coaster HDB30R	Caetano Optimo II	C21F	1993	
L64YJF	Toyota Coaster HZB50R	Caetano Optimo III	C21F	1993	

Livery: White, red, and blue

Regular visitors to the coach park for the Grand National will be aware of the high numbers of coaches that attend. Photographed arriving is Owen's G851VAY, a Dennis Javelin with Duple 320 bodywork. It also carries the Travelmaster name used by Owens. *Graham Ashworth*

PMT sold the Paramount Leisure coach business to Leons of Stafford in January 1994, with many of the coaches numbered in the 15-42 series. STL24 was formerly in the Paramount fleet, but has been retained for the X64 Hanley-Shrewsbury service, that is jointly operated with Midland Red North. The vehicle is a 1983 Plaxton-bodied Leyland Tiger, shown here leaving Shrewsbury bus station on that service. *Ken Crawley*

PMT has a large fleet of Mercedes-Benz L608Ds, mostly carrying PMT conversions to their Hanbridge style and purchased new from PMT Engineering. However, MMM212 (C710JMB) shown here, has a Reeve Burgess conversion and was taken over with the Crosville business in February 1990. *Phillip Stephenson*

PMT

PMT Ltd, 33 Woodhouse Street, Stoke-on-Trent, Staffordshire, ST4 1ER

A member of Badgerline Group plc.

Depots: Adderley Green, Biddulph; Scotia Road, Burslem; Brookhouse Industrial Estate, Cheadle; Liverpool Road, Chester; Second Avenue, Crewe Gates Farm, Crewe; Platt Street, Dukinfield; Bus Station, Ellesmere Port; Rooth Street, Heaton Norris; Pasture Road, Moreton; Liverpool Road, Newcastle-under-Lyme and New Chester Road, Rock Ferry.

CWW14	C967VLS	Volkswagen LT28	Scott	B14F	1986	Ex C & M, Aintree, 1992
STL24	ERF24Y	Leyland Tiger TRCTL11/3R	Plaxton Paramount 3500	C53F	1983	
STL43	E43JRF	Leyland Tiger TRCTL11/3R	Plaxton Paramount 3500 III	C53F	1988	
STL44	E44JRF	Leyland Tiger TRCTL11/3R	Plaxton Paramount 3500 III	C53F	1988	
MMM50	B232AFV	Mercedes-Benz L307D	Reeve Burgess	M12	1985	Ex Landliner, Birkenhead, 1990
SLL80	NED433W	Leyland Leopard PSU3E/4R	Plaxton Supreme IV	C53F	1981	Ex Turner, Brown Edge, 1988
MMM88	C108SFP	Mercedes-Benz L307D	Reeve Burgess	M12	1985	Ex Goldcrest, Birkenhead, 1990
MMM89	F660EBU	Mercedes-Benz 609D	North West CS	C24F	1988	Ex Landliner, Birkenhead, 1990
MMM97	D176VRP	Mercedes-Benz L608D	Alexander	B20F	1986	Ex Milton Keynes Citybus, 1992
MMM98	D185VRP	Mercedes-Benz L608D	Alexander	B20F	1986	Ex Milton Keynes Citybus, 1992
MMM99	C683LGE	Mercedes-Benz L608D	Reeve Burgess	B20F	1985	Ex Strathclyde, 1991
MMM100	F100UEH	Mercedes-Benz 609D	PMT	C24F	1989	
MMM101	G101EVT	Mercedes-Benz L307D	PMT	C21F	1990	
MMM102	F452YHF	Mercedes-Benz 811D	North West CS	C24F	1989	Ex C & M, Aintree, 1992
MHR103	D503ERE	Freight Rover Sherpa	PMT Bursley	C20F	1987	
MMM104	F713OFH	Mercedes-Benz 307D	North West CS	M12	1989	Ex van, 1992
IFF105	J328RVT	Iveco Daily 49.10	Reeve Burgess Beaver	C29F	1991	Ex Roseville Taxis, Newcastle, 1993
MRP106	E106LVT	Renault-Dodge S56	PMT	C22F	1988	
MMM107	XRF2X	Mercedes-Benz L307D	Devon Conversions	M12	1982	Ex Kelly, Lower Gornal, 1985
MRP108	D162LTA	Renault-Dodge S56	Reeve Burgess	B23F	1987	Ex Cardiff, 1994
MMM109	F217OFB	Mercedes-Benz 307D	North West CS	M12	1989	Ex van, 1992
MHR111	D111DEH	Freight Rover Sherpa	PMT Bursley	M15	1986	
MMM112	YRE472Y	Mercedes-Benz L307D	Reeve Burgess	M12	1983	
MMM114	G805AAD	Mercedes-Benz 308	North West CS	M12	1989	Ex van, 1992
MMM115	XRF1X	Mercedes-Benz 608D	PMT	M21L	1984	
MMM116	FXI8653	Mercedes-Benz 608D	PMT	M21L	1984	
MMM117	B117OBF	Mercedes-Benz L608D	PMT	B19F	1984	
MMM118	C684LGE	Mercedes-Benz L608D	Alexander AM	B20F	1986	Ex Strathclyde, 1991
MMM119	B119RRE	Mercedes-Benz L608D	PMT	B19F	1985	

MMM120-159 Mercedes-Benz L608D PMT Hanbridge B20F 1985-86

120	C120VBF	128	C128VRE	137	C137VRE	145	C145WRE	153	D153BEH
121	C121VRE	130	C130VRE	138	C138VRE	146	C146WRE	154	D154BEH
122	C122VRE	131	C131VRE	139	C139VRE	147	C147WRE	155	D155BEH
123	C123VRE	132	C132VRE	140	C140VRE	148	C148WRE	156	D156BEH
124	C124VRE	133	C133VRE	141	C141VRE	149	C149WRE	157	D157BEH
125	C125VRE	134	C134VRE	142	C142VRE	150	C150WRE	158	D158BEH
126	C126VRE	135	C135VRE	143	C143VRE	151	C151WRE	159	D159BEH
127	C127VRE	136	C136VRE	144	C144VRE	152	D152BEH		

MFF162-171 Ford Transit 190D PMT B16F 1986

162	C162VRE	164	C164VRE	168	C168VRE	170	D170BEH	171	D171BEH
163	C163VRE							

MFF172	D534HNW	Ford Transit VE6	Carlyle	B16F	1987	Ex C & M, Aintree, 1992
MFF174	C172WVT	Ford Transit 190D	Robin Hood	B16F	1986	
MFF175	C173WVT	Ford Transit 190D	Robin Hood	B16F	1986	
MFF176	C176WVT	Ford Transit 190D	Robin Hood	B16F	1986	
MFF177	C486TAY	Ford Transit 190D	Dormobile	B16F	1985	Ex Stonier, 1994

MMM180-189 Mercedes-Benz L608D PMT Hanbridge B20F 1986

180	D180BEH	182	D182BEH	184	D184BEH	186	D186BEH	188	D188BEH
181	D181BEH	183	D183BEH	185	D185BEH	187	D187BEH	189	D189BEH

MMM190	C124LHS	Mercedes-Benz L608D		Reeve Burgess		B20F	1986	Ex Strathclyde, 1991	
MMM191	D118PGA	Mercedes-Benz L608D		Reeve Burgess		B19F	1986	Ex Strathclyde, 1991	
MMM192	D119PGA	Mercedes-Benz L608D		Imperial		B23F	1986	Ex Strathclyde, 1991	

MMM193-197 Mercedes-Benz L608D — PMT Hanbridge — B19F — 1986 — Ex Strathclyde, 1991

193	D120PGA	**194**	D121PGA	**195**	D122PGA	**196**	D123PGA	**197**	D124PGA

MMM199-209 Mercedes-Benz L608D — Alexander — B20F — 1986 — Ex Milton Keynes Citybus, 1992

199	D159VRP	**202**	D165VRP	**204**	D180VRP	**206**	D187VRP	**208**	D178VRP
200	D160VRP	**203**	D179VRP	**205**	D186VRP	**207**	D157VRP	**209**	D184VRP
201	D162VRP								

MMM210	C706JMB	Mercedes-Benz L608D		Reeve Burgess		B19F	1986	Ex Crosville, 1990	
MMM211	C709JMB	Mercedes-Benz L608D		Reeve Burgess		B19F	1986	Ex Crosville, 1990	
MMM212	C710JMB	Mercedes-Benz L608D		Reeve Burgess		B19F	1986	Ex Crosville, 1990	
MMM213	C711JMB	Mercedes-Benz L608D		Reeve Burgess		B19F	1986	Ex Crosville, 1990	
MMM214	CSC818W	Mercedes-Benz L508D		Reeve Burgess		B20F	1981	Ex Stonier, 1994	

MPC224-230 MCW MetroRider MF150/118 — MCW — B25F — 1988 — Ex Crosville, 1990

224	F88CWG	**226**	F106CWG	**228**	F108CWG	**229**	F109CWG	**230**	F110CWG
225	F95CWG	**227**	F107CWG						

MPC231	L231NRE	Optare MetroRider	Optare	B31F	1994		
SRG280	NLJ821G	Bristol RELL6G	Eastern Coach Works	B53F	1971	Ex Pennine Blue, 1993	
SRG281	TUO263J	Bristol RELL6G	Eastern Coach Works	B53F	1971	Ex Pennine Blue, 1993	
SNL287	SFA287R	Leyland National 11351A/1R		B52F	1977		
SNL288	WUH172T	Leyland National 11351A/1R		B49F	1979	Ex Rhondda, 1992	
SNL289	WUH173T	Leyland National 11351A/1R		B49F	1979	Ex Rhondda, 1992	
SNG297	EMB358S	Leyland National 11351A/1R		B49F	1978	Ex Crosville, 1990	
SNG298	GMB377T	Leyland National 11351A/1R		B49F	1978	Ex Crosville, 1990	
SNG299	KMA407T	Leyland National 11351A/1R		B49F	1979	Ex Crosville, 1990	

Opposite, top: **This Optare-bodied DAF SB220 of PMT, SAD802, H802GRE, is seen working service 320 to Hanley and passing through the Cheshire countryside. This vehicle is one of a batch of nine - all fitted with high backed seats making them suitable for a wide variety of duties.** *Cliff Beeton*

Opposite, bottom: **An unusual vehicle for a major operator is PMT MXP449, K449XRF. This is a Talbot Pullman with 18-seat bodywork. TBP in Birmingham, took over the licence for bodywork on Talbot tri-axle vehicles from Talbot's own body building division. This vehicle was new in October 1992 and is allocated to Red Rider Moreton garage on the Wirral.** *Phillip Stephenson*

Leyland Nationals are now rare in the PMT fleet. There are seven remaining, only two of which were purchased new, and these are currently delicensed. Still very active, though, are two vehicles purchased from Rhondda in 1992 and originally new to Jones of Aberdare. SNL289 is seen here at Burslem garage waiting to take up duties on Route 26. *Cliff Beeton*

IWC310-318   Leyland Swift LBM6T/2RS   PMT Knype   DP37F*   1988-89   *315-8 are DP35F

310	F310REH	312	F312REH	315	F315REH	317	F317REH	318	G318YVT
311	F311REH	313	F313REH	316	F316REH				

IWC320	E342NFA	Leyland Swift LBM6T/2RS	PMT Knype	DP37F	1988 Ex PMT demonstrator, 1988
IPC321	L321HRE	Optare MetroRider	Optare	DP30F	1993
IPC322	L269GBU	Optare MetroRider	Optare	B29F	1993
IPC323	L323NRE	Optare MetroRider	Optare	B29F	1994

IMM330-353   Mercedes-Benz 811D   PMT Ami   B28F   1989-90

330	G330XRE	335	G335XRE	340	G340XRE	345	G345CBF	350	G550ERF
331	G331XRE	336	G336XRE	341	G341XRE	346	G346CBF	351	H351HRF
332	G332XRE	337	G337XRE	342	G342CBF	347	G347ERF	352	H352HRF
333	G333XRE	338	G338XRE	343	G343CBF	348	G348ERF	353	H353HRF
334	G334XRE	339	G339XRE	344	G344CBF	349	G349ERF		

IMM354	H354HVT	Mercedes-Benz 811D	Reeve Burgess Beaver	B31F	1990
IMM355	H355HVT	Mercedes-Benz 811D	Reeve Burgess Beaver	B31F	1990
IMM356	H356HVT	Mercedes-Benz 811D	Reeve Burgess Beaver	B33F	1990
IMM357	H357HVT	Mercedes-Benz 811D	Reeve Burgess Beaver	B33F	1990

IMM358-363   Mercedes-Benz 811D   PMT Ami   B29F   1990

358	H358JRE	360	H160JRE	361	H361JRE	362	H362JRE	363	H363JRE
359	H359JRE								

IMM364	E39KRE	Mercedes-Benz L811D	PMT	B25F	1988 Ex van, 1990
IMM365	G495FFA	Mercedes-Benz 811D	PMT Ami	B28F	1990

The X38 service from Hanley to Derby is operated by PMT on Saturdays only. Nevertheless, the photographer managed to photograph IWC320, E342NFA, which is a PMT Knype-bodied Leyland Swift, on this service. These vehicles all now have high backed seating and entered service in 1988 and 1989. IWC320 was originally a demonstrator while 314 was withdrawn from passenger service for use as a driver-trainer. *Keith Grimes*

PMT's own 29-seat Ami bodywork is fitted to this Mercedes-Benz 811D. It is allocated to Chester garage in the Crosville division and is seen here in Chester bus exchange. *Richard Eversden*

Vehicles operated outside the Potteries by PMT carry the legend Red Rider. The vehicle shown here is departing from Stockport bus station on a local service. IMM356, H356HVT, is one of a small batch of Mercedes-Benz 811Ds with Reeve Burgess Beaver bodywork. *Keith Grimes*

IMM366-371　　Mercedes-Benz 811D　　PMT Ami B29F　　1991

366	H366LFA	**368**	H368LFA	**369**	H369LFA	**370**	H370LFA	**371**	H371LFA
367	H367LFA								

IMM372	H372MEH	Mercedes-Benz 811D	Whittaker-Europa	B31F	1991	
IMM373	H373MVT	Mercedes-Benz 811D	PMT Ami	B29F	1991	
IMM374	K374BRE	Mercedes-Benz 811D	Autobus Classique	B29F	1992	
IMM375	K375BRE	Mercedes-Benz 811D	Autobus Classique	B29F	1992	
IMM376	J920HGD	Mercedes-Benz 709D		B29F	1991	Ex Stonier, 1994
MHF394	D77YRF	Freight Rover Sherpa	Dormobile	B16F	1986	Ex Pennine Blue, 1993
MHF395	D146NON	Freight Rover Sherpa	Carlyle	B20F	1987	Ex Stonier, 1994
MHF396	D196NON	Freight Rover Sherpa	Carlyle	B20F	1987	Ex Stonier, 1994
MHF397	D259OOJ	Freight Rover Sherpa	Carlyle	B20F	1987	Ex Crosville, 1990
MHR398	D714PTU	Freight Rover Sherpa	Dormobile	B16F	1986	Ex Crosville, 1990
MHR399	D718PTU	Freight Rover Sherpa	Dormobile	B16F	1986	Ex Crosville, 1990
MHR400	D723PTU	Freight Rover Sherpa	Dormobile	B16F	1986	Ex Crosville, 1990
MHF401	D401ERE	Freight Rover Sherpa	PMT Bursley	B20F	1987	
MHR402	D731PTU	Freight Rover Sherpa	Dormobile	B16F	1986	Ex Crosville, 1990
MHR403	D736PTU	Freight Rover Sherpa	Dormobile	B16F	1986	Ex Crosville, 1990
MHR405	D405ERE	Freight Rover Sherpa	PMT Bursley	B20F	1987	
MHR406	D406ERE	Freight Rover Sherpa	PMT Bursley	B20F	1987	
MHF407	D407ERE	Freight Rover Sherpa	PMT Bursley	B20F	1987	
MHF408	D408ERE	Freight Rover Sherpa	PMT Bursley	B20F	1987	
MHF409	D409ERE	Freight Rover Sherpa	PMT Bursley	B20F	1987	
MHR410	D767PTU	Freight Rover Sherpa	Dormobile	B16F	1986	Ex Crosville, 1990
MHR411	D775PTU	Freight Rover Sherpa	Dormobile	B16F	1986	Ex Crosville, 1990
MHF412	D412FEH	Freight Rover Sherpa	PMT Bursley	B20F	1987	
MHR413	D413FEH	Freight Rover Sherpa	PMT Bursley	B20F	1987	
MHR414	D414FEH	Freight Rover Sherpa	PMT Bursley	B20F	1987	
MHF415	D776PTU	Freight Rover Sherpa	Dormobile	B16F	1986	Ex Crosville, 1990
MHF416	D416FEH	Freight Rover Sherpa	PMT Bursley	B20F	1987	
MHR418	D783RFM	Freight Rover Sherpa	Dormobile	B16F	1986	Ex Crosville, 1990
MHR419	D419FEH	Freight Rover Sherpa	PMT Bursley	B20F	1987	
MHR420	D420FEH	Freight Rover Sherpa	PMT Bursley	B20F	1987	
MHR421	D788RFM	Freight Rover Sherpa	Dormobile	B16F	1986	Ex Crosville, 1990
MHR422	E722HBF	Freight Rover Sherpa	PMT Bursley	B20F	1987	
MHF423	E723HBF	Freight Rover Sherpa	PMT Bursley	B20F	1987	
MHR424	E724HBF	Freight Rover Sherpa	PMT Bursley	B20F	1987	
MHF425	E725HBF	Freight Rover Sherpa	PMT Bursley	B20F	1987	
MHF426	E726HBF	Freight Rover Sherpa	PMT Bursley	B20F	1987	
MHF427	E727HBF	Freight Rover Sherpa	PMT Bursley	B20F	1987	
MHF428	E728HBF	Freight Rover Sherpa	PMT Bursley	B20F	1987	

MMM430-448　　Mercedes-Benz 709D　　Plaxton Beaver　　B24F　　1992

430	J430WFA	**434**	K434XRF	**438**	K438XRF	**442**	K442XRF	**446**	K446XRF
431	J431WFA	**435**	K435XRF	**439**	K439XRF	**443**	K443XRF	**447**	K447XRF
432	K432XRF	**436**	K436XRF	**440**	K440XRF	**444**	K544XRF	**448**	K448XRF
433	K433XRF	**437**	K437XRF	**441**	K441XRF	**445**	K445XRF		

MXP449	K449XRF	Peugeot-Talbot Pullman	TBP	B18F	1992	
MMM450	E791CCA	Mercedes-Benz 609D	PMT	B20F	1988	Ex Roberts, Bootle, 1992

MMM451-466　　Mercedes-Benz L608D　　PMT Hanbridge　　B20F　　1987-88

451	D451ERE	**454**	D454ERE	**457**	D457ERE	**460**	E460HBF	**464**	E764HBF
452	D452ERE	**455**	D455ERE	**458**	D458ERE	**461**	E761HBF	**465**	E765HBF
453	D453ERE	**456**	D456ERE	**459**	D459ERE	**462**	E762HBF	**466**	E766HBF

MMM467	E767HBF	Mercedes-Benz 709D	PMT	B21F	1988	
MMM468	E768HBF	Mercedes-Benz 609D	PMT	B20F	1987	
MMM469	E769HBF	Mercedes-Benz 609D	Reeve Burgess	B20F	1987	
MMM470	E470MVT	Mercedes-Benz 709D	PMT	B23F	1988	
MMM471	E471MVT	Mercedes-Benz 609D	PMT	B20F	1988	
MMM472	F472RBF	Mercedes-Benz 609D	PMT	B20F	1988	
MMM473	F473RBF	Mercedes-Benz 609D	PMT	B20F	1988	
MMM474	E41JRF	Mercedes-Benz 709D	PMT	B23F	1988	
MMM475	F475VEH	Mercedes-Benz 609D	PMT	B20F	1989	
MMM476	E831ETY	Mercedes-Benz 609D	Reeve Burgess Beaver	B20F	1988	Ex Vasey, Ashington, 1990

MMM477	G477ERF	Mercedes-Benz 609D	PMT	B20F	1990	
MMM478	G478ERF	Mercedes-Benz 609D	PMT	B20F	1990	
MMM479	E384XCA	Mercedes-Benz 609D	PMT	B24F	1987	Ex Dennis's, Ashton, 1990
MMM480	H180JRE	Mercedes-Benz 709D	PMT	B20F	1990	
MMM481	H481JRE	Mercedes-Benz 709D	PMT	B25F	1990	
MMM482	H482JRE	Mercedes-Benz 609D	Whittaker Europa	B20F	1990	
MMM483	H483JRE	Mercedes-Benz 609D	Whittaker Europa	B20F	1990	
MMM484	J484PVT	Mercedes-Benz 709D	PMT	B25F	1991	
MMM485	J485PVT	Mercedes-Benz 709D	Whittaker (PMT)	B25F	1992	
MMM486	J486PVT	Mercedes-Benz 709D	Whittaker (PMT)	B25F	1992	

MMM487-498   Mercedes-Benz 709D   Dormobile Routemaker   B24F*   1993   *488/9 are B27F

487	K487CVT	490	K490CVT	493	L493HRE	495	L495HRE	497	L497HRE
488	K488CVT	491	K491CVT	494	L494HRE	496	L496HRE	498	L498HRE
489	K489CVT	492	K492CVT						

MRP501	E801HBF	Renault-Dodge S56	PMT	B25F	1987

MRP502-529   Renault-Dodge S56   Alexander AM   B20F*   1987   *527/8 are B25F; 529 is B23F

502	E802HBF	508	E808HBF	514	E814HBF	520	E820HBF	525	E825HBF
503	E803HBF	509	E809HBF	515	E815HBF	521	E821HBF	526	E826HBF
504	E804HBF	510	E810HBF	516	E816HBF	522	E822HBF	527	E527JRE
505	E805HBF	511	E811HBF	517	E817HBF	523	E823HBF	528	E528JRE
506	E806HBF	512	E812HBF	518	E818HBF	524	E824HBF	529	E529JRE
507	E807HBF	513	E813HBF	519	E819HBF					

MRP530	E526NEH	Renault-Dodge S56	PMT	B25F	1988	
MRP531	F531UVT	Renault-Dodge S56	PMT	B25F	1989	
MRP532	G532CVT	Renault-Dodge S56	PMT	B25F	1990	
MRP533	D858LND	Renault-Dodge S56	Northern Counties	B20F	1986	Ex Stonier, 1994
MRP534	D809MNY	Renault-Dodge S56	Northern Counties	B24F	1987	Ex Stonier, 1994
MRP535	D669SEM	Renault-Dodge S56	Northern Counties	B22F	1986	Ex Stonier, 1994
MRP536	D671SEM	Renault-Dodge S56	Northern Counties	B22F	1986	Ex Stonier, 1994
MRP537	D848LND	Renault-Dodge S56	Northern Counties	B20F	1986	Ex Pennine Blue, 1993
MRP538	D974TKC	Renault-Dodge S56	Northern Counties	B22F	1987	Ex Pennine Blue, 1993
MRP540	D710TWM	Renault-Dodge S56	Northern Counties	B22F	1987	Ex Pennine Blue, 1993
MMM550	H834GLD	Mercedes-Benz 609D	North West CS	B19F	1990	Ex Capital Coaches, 1994
MMM551	H834GLD	Mercedes-Benz 609D	North West CS	B19F	1990	Ex Capital Coaches, 1994
MMM552	H834GLD	Mercedes-Benz 609D	North West CS	B19F	1990	Ex Capital Coaches, 1994

MMM553-558   Mercedes-Benz 709D   Marshall   B24F   1994

553	L553LVT	555	L455LVT	556	L556LVT	557	L557LVT	558	L558LVT
554	L554LVT								

DVG601	OEH601M	Bristol VRT/SL2/6G	Eastern Coach Works	H43/31F	1974	
DVG606	WDM341R	Bristol VRT/SL3/501(6LXB)	Eastern Coach Works	H43/31F	1977	Ex Crosville, 1990
DVG607	UDM450V	Bristol VRT/SL3/501(6LXB)	Eastern Coach Works	H43/31F	1980	Ex Crosville, 1990
DVG608	VCA452W	Bristol VRT/SL3/501(6LXB)	Eastern Coach Works	H43/31F	1980	Ex Crosville, 1990
DVG609	VCA464W	Bristol VRT/SL3/501(6LXB)	Eastern Coach Works	H43/31F	1980	Ex Crosville, 1990
DVG610	WTU465W	Bristol VRT/SL3/501(6LXB)	Eastern Coach Works	H43/31F	1980	Ex Crosville, 1990
DVG611	WTU472W	Bristol VRT/SL3/501(6LXB)	Eastern Coach Works	H43/31F	1980	Ex Crosville, 1990
DVG612	WTU481W	Bristol VRT/SL3/501(6LXB)	Eastern Coach Works	H43/31F	1981	Ex Crosville, 1990
DVG613	WTU482W	Bristol VRT/SL3/501(6LXB)	Eastern Coach Works	H43/31F	1981	Ex Crosville, 1990
DVG614	WTU483W	Bristol VRT/SL3/501(6LXB)	Eastern Coach Works	H43/31F	1981	Ex Crosville, 1990
DVG615	DCA526X	Bristol VRT/SL3/501(6LXB)	Eastern Coach Works	H43/31F	1981	Ex Crosville, 1990

DVG616-621   Bristol VRT/SL3/6LXB   Eastern Coach Works   H43/31F   1979   Ex Thames Transit, 1989

616	YBW487V	618	YBW489V	619	EJO490V	620	EJO491V	621	EJO492V
617	YBW488V								

DVG622	507EXA	Bristol VRT/SL2/6G	Eastern Coach Works	O43/31F	1974	
DVG623	JWT761V	Bristol VRT/SL3/6LXB	Eastern Coach Works	H43/31F	1979	Ex West Yorkshire, 1989
DVG624	AHU515V	Bristol VRT/SL3/6LXB	Eastern Coach Works	H43/31F	1980	Ex City Line, 1994
DVG625	AHW203V	Bristol VRT/SL3/6LXB	Eastern Coach Works	H43/31F	1980	Ex City Line, 1994

DVL634	FTU383T	Bristol VRT/SL3/501	Eastern Coach Works	H43/31F	1978	Ex Pennine, 1993
DVL635	UMB333R	Bristol VRT/SL3/501	Eastern Coach Works	H43/31F	1977	Ex Crosville, 1990
DVL636	UMB340R	Bristol VRT/SL3/501	Eastern Coach Works	H43/31F	1977	Ex Crosville, 1990
DVL639	WDM348R	Bristol VRT/SL3/501	Eastern Coach Works	H43/31F	1977	Ex Crosville, 1990
DVL640	ODM409V	Bristol VRT/SL3/501	Eastern Coach Works	H43/31F	1979	Ex Crosville, 1990
DVL641	PCA420V	Bristol VRT/SL3/501	Eastern Coach Works	H43/31F	1979	Ex Crosville, 1990
DVL642	PCA421V	Bristol VRT/SL3/501	Eastern Coach Works	H43/31F	1979	Ex Crosville, 1990
DVL643	RLG430V	Bristol VRT/SL3/501	Eastern Coach Works	H43/31F	1980	Ex Crosville, 1990
DVL644	RMA443V	Bristol VRT/SL3/501	Eastern Coach Works	H43/31F	1980	Ex Crosville, 1990
DVL645	WTU488W	Bristol VRT/SL3/501	Eastern Coach Works	H43/31F	1981	Ex Crosville, 1990
DVL646	WTU489W	Bristol VRT/SL3/501	Eastern Coach Works	H43/31F	1981	Ex Crosville, 1990
DVL647	WTU491W	Bristol VRT/SL3/501	Eastern Coach Works	H43/31F	1981	Ex Crosville, 1990
DVL661	CBV3S	Bristol VRT/SL3/501	Eastern Coach Works	H43/31F	1977	Ex Ribble, 1982
DVL667	URF667S	Bristol VRT/SL3/501	Eastern Coach Works	H43/31F	1978	
DVL674	URF674S	Bristol VRT/SL3/501	Eastern Coach Works	H43/31F	1978	
DVL677	URF677S	Bristol VRT/SL3/501	Eastern Coach Works	H43/31F	1978	
DVL680	YBF680S	Bristol VRT/SL3/501	Eastern Coach Works	H43/31F	1978	
DVL685	YBF685S	Bristol VRT/SL3/501	Eastern Coach Works	H43/31F	1978	
DVL689	BRF689T	Bristol VRT/SL3/501	Eastern Coach Works	H43/31F	1978	
DVL693	BRF693T	Bristol VRT/SL3/501	Eastern Coach Works	H43/31F	1978	

DVL701-732

Bristol VRT/SL3/501 Eastern Coach Works H43/31F* 1979-80 705 is DVC705
*706/11-3/8/20-8/30/2 are DPH39/28F

701	GRF701V	**709**	GRF709V	**715**	GRF715V	**721**	MFA721V	**727**	NEH727W
703	GRF703V	**710**	GRF710V	**716**	GRF716V	**722**	MFA722V	**728**	NEH728W
704	GRF704V	**711**	GRF711V	**717**	MFA717V	**723**	MFA723V	**729**	NEH729W
706	GRF706V	**712**	GRF712V	**718**	MFA718V	**724**	NEH724W	**730**	NEH730W
707	GRF707V	**713**	GRF713V	**719**	MFA719V	**725**	NEH725W	**731**	NEH731W
708	GRF708V	**714**	GRF714V	**720**	MFA720V	**726**	NEH726W	**732**	NEH732W

Opposite, top: **DOG735, A735GFA,** is an Eastern Coach Works-bodied Leyland Olympian in the PMT fleet. These vehicles are nearly all allocated to Newcastle or Adderley Green garages and have now given just over ten years of service to the company. *Cliff Beeton*

Opposite, bottom: In contrast to DOG735, DOG742 is painted in Turner's livery. The painting style is different from that used by this former independent, but the colours are the same. This vehicle is actually travelling to Brown Edge, where Turners' garage was located and while the only double-deck in the fleet in this livery, four minibuses and a Dennis Dart also carry the Turners livery. *Cliff Beeton*

In common with many companies, PMT operate an open-top double decker on special services, excursions etc. Although not carrying a fleet number, 507EXA is DVG622 in the PMT fleet while this Eastern Coach Works-bodied Bristol VRT was formerly registered GBF78N. A frequent use for the vehicle was in connection with Chatterley Whitfield Mining Museum. Now that this has closed, alternative uses may be sought. *Cliff Beeton*

DOG733-747

DOG733-747		Leyland Olympian ONLXB/1R		Eastern Coach Works		H45/32F		1983-84		

733	A733GFA	736	A736GFA	739	A739GFA	742	A742GFA	745	A745JRE
734	A734GFA	737	A737GFA	740	A740GFA	743	A743JRE	746	A746JRE
735	A735GFA	738	A738GFA	741	A741GFA	744	A744JRE	747	A747JRE

DOG748	EWY78Y	Leyland Olympian ONLXB/1R	Roe	H47/29F	1983	Ex Turner, Brown Edge, 1988
DOG749	EWY79Y	Leyland Olympian ONLXB/1R	Roe	H47/29F	1983	Ex Turner, Brown Edge, 1988
DOC750	GFM101X	Leyland Olympian ONCL10/1RZ	Eastern Coach Works	H45/32F	1982	Ex Crosville, 1990
DOC751	GFM102X	Leyland Olympian ONCL10/1RZ	Eastern Coach Works	H45/32F	1982	Ex Crosville, 1990
DOC752	GFM103X	Leyland Olympian ONCL10/1RZ	Eastern Coach Works	H45/32F	1982	Ex Crosville, 1990

DOC753-762

DOC753-762	Leyland Olympian ONCL11/1RZ	Leyland	H47/29F*	*756-762 are DPH43/29F

753	G753XRE	755	G755XRE	757	G757XRE	759	G759XRE	761	G761XRE
754	G754XRE	756	G756XRE	758	G758XRE	760	G760XRE	762	G762XRE

DOG763-783

DOG763-783	Leyland Olympian ONLXB/1R	Eastern Coach Works	H45/32F	1982-83 Ex Crosville, 1990

763	GFM104X	768	KFM111Y	772	KFM115Y	776	MTU124Y	780	A138SMA
764	GFM105X	769	KFM112Y	773	MTU120Y	777	MTU125Y	781	A143SMA
765	GFM106X	770	KFM113Y	774	MTU122Y	778	A136SMA	782	A144SMA
766	GFM108X	771	KFM114Y	775	MTU123Y	779	A137SMA	783	A145SMA
767	GFM109X								

DOG784-799

DOG784-799	Leyland Olympian ONLXB/1R	Eastern Coach Works	H45/32F	1984-85 Ex Crosville, 1990

784	A146UDM	788	A159UDM	791	A162VDM	794	A165VDM	797	A168VFM
785	A156UDM	789	A160UDM	792	A163VDM	795	A166VFM	798	A169VFM
786	A157UDM	790	A161VDM	793	A164VDM	796	A167VFM	799	A170VFM
787	A158UDM								

Many Eastern Coach Works-bodied Leyland Olympians passed to PMT from Crosville in 1990. One such vehicle is DOG765, GFM106X, seen here at Heswall. The majority of these vehicles is still to be seen in the Crosville division, although several have been transferred to Staffordshire garages. Those in the former Crosville area carry Crosville fleetnames in place of PMT or Red Rider. An additional 'Crosville' also appears on the front of this vehicle. *Phillip Stephenson*

Opposite: **Dedicated vehicles for a particular route have been used by PMT quite extensively. DOC760, G760XRE, is one of several vehicles operating the Hanley-Crewe service. It is an all-Leyland Olympian, one of a batch of seven fitted with high-back seating. The vehicle was photographed in Crewe.** *Roy Marshall*

An example not only of a route dedicated vehicle, but of a special route livery is seen DOG734, A734GFA. This vehicle is one of the batch of Eastern Coach Works-bodied Leyland Olympians new to PMT in 1983. It is allocated to Newcastle for working Route 17 Bradwell-Hanley through Wolstanton on which service it was photographed. *Phillip Stehenson*

SAD801-809 — DAF SB220LC550 — Optare Delta — DP48F — 1990

801	H801GRE	803	H803GRE	805	H805GRE	807	H807GRE	809	H809GRE
802	H802GRE	804	H804GRE	806	H806GRE	808	H808GRE		

SLC849	F608WBV	Leyland Lynx LX112L10ZR1S	Leyland Lynx	B52F	1988	Ex Westbus, Ashford, 1993
SLC850	G136YRY	Leyland Lynx LX112L10ZR1R	Leyland Lynx	B51F	1990	Ex Westbus, Ashford, 1993

SLC851-861 — Leyland Lynx LX2R11C15Z4S — Leyland Lynx — DP48F — 1990

851	H851GRE	854	H854GRE	856	H856GRE	858	H858GRE	860	H860GRE
852	H852GRE	855	H855GRE	857	H857GRE	859	H859GRE	861	H861GRE
853	H853GRE								

SDC862	L862HFA	Dennis Lance 11SDA3112	Northern Counties Paladin	DP47F	1993	
DFL884	WJN352J	Daimler Fleetline CRL6-33	Northern Counties	H49/33F	1972	Ex Pennine Blue, 1993
DFL885	XUF387K	Daimler Fleetline CRL6	Eastern Coach Works	H43/31F	1972	Ex Pennine Blue, 1993
DAL886	SUG574M	Leyland Atlantean AN68/1R	Roe	H45/33D	1974	Ex Pennine Blue, 1993
DAL887	WWM926W	Leyland Atlantean AN68B/1R	Willowbrook	H45/33F	1981	Ex Pennine Blue, 1993
DAL888	WWM928W	Leyland Atlantean AN68B/1R	Willowbrook	H45/33F	1981	Ex Pennine Blue, 1993
DAL889	WWM932W	Leyland Atlantean AN68B/1R	Willowbrook	H45/33F	1981	Ex Pennine Blue, 1993
DAL890	AFY180X	Leyland Atlantean AN68B/1R	Willowbrook	H45/33F	1981	Ex Pennine Blue, 1993
DOG891	A171VFM	Leyland Olympian ON6LXB/1RT	Eastern Coach Works	H45/32F	1984	Ex Crosville, 1990
DOG892	B181BLG	Leyland Olympian ON6LXB/1HI	Eastern Coach Works	H45/32F	1984	Ex Crosville, 1990
DOG893	B182BLG	Leyland Olympian ON6LXB/1RT	Eastern Coach Works	H45/32F	1984	Ex Crosville, 1990
DOG894	B188BLG	Leyland Olympian ON6LXB/1RT	Eastern Coach Works	H45/32F	1985	Ex Crosville, 1990
DOG895	B195BLG	Leyland Olympian ON6LXB/1RT	Eastern Coach Works	H45/32F	1985	Ex Crosville, 1990

In August 1990, PMT received a batch of nine DAF SB220s with Optare Delta bodywork. Most of these were allocated to Burslem and have remained there. The last three have seen service at Chester, although they are now back in the Potteries. SAD807 was photographed while at Chester working Route 3 to Rivacre Brow. *Cliff Beeton*

The North Midland Bus Handbook

Eleven Leyland Lynx entered service in August 1990, alongside the Optare Deltas. These too were also allocated to Burslem, and for some time operated as a separate Lynx unit from there. This separation has now ceased but these vehicles predominantly are to be seen on Route 24. SLC853, H853GRE, is arriving at Talke Pits in this view. *Cliff Beeton*

A recent arrival in the PMT fleet is a Dennis Lance SDC862, L862HFA. Fitted with Northern Counties Paladin bodywork, it was photographed while on a test drive through Skelmersdale. It is now allocated to duties on the Wirral as the use of the Crosville name might suggest. *Graham Ashworth*

DOG896	B199DTU	Leyland Olympian ON6LXB/1RT	Eastern Coach Works	H45/32F	1985	Ex Crosville, 1990	
DOG897	B200DTU	Leyland Olympian ONLXB/1R	Eastern Coach Works	DPH42/32F	1985	Ex Crosville, 1990	
DOG898	B201DTU	Leyland Olympian ONLXB/1R	Eastern Coach Works	DPH42/32F	1985	Ex Crosville, 1990	
DOG899	B202DTU	Leyland Olympian ONLXB/1R	Eastern Coach Works	DPH42/32F	1985	Ex Crosville, 1990	
D900	WVT900S	Foden/NC 6LXB	Northern Counties	H43/31F	1978		

IDC901-918
Dennis Dart 9.5SDL3011   Plaxton Pointer   DP35F   1991-92

901	J901SEH	**905**	J905SEH	**909**	J909SEH	**913**	J913SEH	**916**	J916SEH
902	J902SEH	**906**	J906SEH	**910**	J910SEH	**914**	J914SEH	**917**	J917SEH
903	J903SEH	**907**	J907SEH	**911**	J911SEH	**915**	J915SEH	**918**	J918SEH
904	J904SEH	**908**	J908SEH	**912**	J912SEH				

IDC919-929
Dennis Dart 9.5SDL3016   Plaxton Pointer   DP35F   1992

919	K919XRF	**922**	K922XRF	**924**	K924XRF	**926**	K926XRF	**928**	K928XRF
920	K920XRF	**923**	K923XRF	**925**	K925XRF	**927**	K927XRF	**929**	K929XRF
921	K921XRF								

IDC930-934
Dennis Dart 9.5SDL3016   Plaxton Pointer   DP35F   1993

930	L930HFA	**931**	L931HFA	**932**	L932HFA	**933**	L933HFA	**934**	L934HFA

IDC935	L935HFA	Dennis Dart 9.5SDL3016	Marshall	DP36F	1993	
IDC936	L936HFA	Dennis Dart 9.5SDL3016	Marshall	DP36F	1993	

IDC937-942
Dennis Dart 9.5SDL3016   Plaxton Pointer   DP35F   1994

937	L937LRF	**939**	L939LRF	**940**	L940LRF	**941**	L941LRF	**942**	L942LRF
938	L938LRF								

Previous Registrations:

FXI8653	B116NBF		XRF1X	B115NBF		XRF2X	GLG830X

Livery: Red and yellow
Turners: MMM430/1, MMM550/1, DOG740/2, IDC928.
Pennine Blue   Vehicles based at Dukinfield

The Dennis Dart with Plaxton Pointer bodywork has been favoured for mid-sized vehicles since 1992. All these vehicles have 35 high-back seating for dual use. Of the first batch of 17 vehicles, all except three were allocated to the Crosville division at Rock Ferry. The second batch is more local and IDC930, L930HFA is one allocated to Newcastle and sports the legend 'The Potteries Connection' in addition to the PMT panel. The photograph was taken in Hanley.
Keith Grimes

The first of a pair of Marshall-bodied Dennis Dart for PMT is seen at Woodside ferry terminal at Birkenhead. IDC935, L935HFA also carries the Crosville names. *Graham Ashworth*

Definition of PMT Fleet Codes:

1st letter - Class

C	Coach
D	Double Deck
S	Single Deck
I	Midibus
M	Minibus

2nd letter - Chassis

A	DAF or Atlantean
B*	Volvo
D	Dart
F	Ford or Fleetline
H	Freight Rover
L	Lynx
M	Mercedes-Benz
N	National
O	Olympian
P	Optare
R	Renault or Bristol RELL
S*	Scania
T	Tiger
V	Bristol VRT
W	Swift
X	Talbot

3rd letter - Engine

A*	AEC
B*	Bedford
C	Cummins
D	DAF
E*	Electric
F	Ford
G	Gardner
L	Leyland
M	Mercedes-Benz
P	Perkins
R	Rover
S*	Scania
V*	Volvo

* Not currently in use.

POTTERIES BUS SERVICE

FA & JE Gilbert, 1 Beard Grove, Carmountside, Abbey Hulton, Stoke on Trent, ST2 8DF

D122TFT	Freight Rover Sherpa	Carlyle	B18F	1986	Ex Derby, 1992

PROCTERS

F Procter & Son Ltd, Dewsbury Road, Fenton, Stoke-on-Trent, Staffordshire, ST4 2HS

Reg	Chassis	Body	Seating	Year	Notes
AFA729S	AEC Reliance 6U3ZR	Duple Dominant II	C57F	1978	
YUT326T	Bristol LH6L	Plaxton Supreme III	C45F	1979	Ex Jalna, Church Gresley, 1981
HRE128V	Leyland Leopard PSU3E/4R	Plaxton Supreme IV Express	C53F	1979	
HRE129V	Leyland Leopard PSU3E/4R	Plaxton Supreme IV Express	C53F	1979	
HIL7624	Leyland Leopard PSU3E/4R	Plaxton Supreme IV Express	C53F	1979	Ex Middleton, Rugeley, 1980
WCK128V	Leyland Leopard PSU3E/4R	Duple Dominant II	C53F	1980	Ex Cumberland, 1988
HIL7623	Leyland Leopard PSU3E/4R	Plaxton Supreme V Express	C53F	1982	
HIL7622	Leyland Tiger TRCTL11/3R	Duple Dominant IV	C57F	1982	
HIL7621	Leyland Tiger TRCTL11/3R	Duple Dominant IV	C57F	1982	
HIL2379	Leyland Tiger TRCTL11/3R	Duple Dominant IV	C57F	1982	
EVT690Y	Ford Transit 190	Deansgate	B12F	1983	
HIL2376	Leyland Royal Tiger RTC	Leyland Doyen	C49FT	1986	
HIL2377	DAF SB2300DHS585	Duple 340	C57F	1986	Ex Smiths, Alcester, 1987
HIL2378	Leyland Tiger TRCTL11/3RZ	Duple 340	C57F	1986	
HIL2375	DAF SB2300DHS585	Duple 340	C53F	1987	
HIL7620	Scania K112CRB	Van Hool Alizée	C51F	1988	Ex Stanley Gath, Dewsbury, 1992
HIL7615	Dennis Javelin 12SDA1907	Duple 320	C57F	1988	
HIL7616	Dennis Javelin 12SDA1907	Duple 320	C57F	1988	
HIL7613	Dennis Javelin 12SDA1907	Duple 320	C57F	1989	
HIL7614	Dennis Javelin 12SDA1907	Duple 320	C57F	1989	
HIL7386	DAF MB230LT615	Van Hool Alizée	C51F	1990	Ex Smiths, Alcester, 1992

Previous Registrations:

HIL2375	D294XCX	HIL7386	G977KJX	HIL7620	E58VHL
HIL2376	C269XRF	HIL7613	F702TBF	HIL7621	WFA210X
HIL2377	C780MVH	HIL7614	F703TBF	HIL7622	WFA209X
HIL2378	C962YBF	HIL7615	E846LRF	HIL7623	WVT107X
HIL2379	ARE508Y	HIL7616	E847LRF	HIL7624	JRE355V

Livery: Blue and cream

Proctors continue to operate a Bristol LH. Of the longer LH6L type it is fitted with a Plaxton Supreme III body. YUT326T is seen in Blackpool's central coach park. *Graham Ashworth*

Operating on service from Stockport bus station is one of Procters' four Dennis Javelins. Each is fitted with Duple bodywork. F703TBF has now received a private index plate, HIL7614 leaving only five older coaches and a minibus carrying standard index marks. *Graham Ashworth*

ROGER HILL COACHES

E R & A Hill, 6 Ennerdale Drive, Congleton, Cheshire, CW12 4FR

XUF398K	Daimler Fleetline CRL6	Eastern Coach Works	H43/31F	1988	Ex Crosville Wales, 1988
HIL3479	Daimler Fleetline CRG6LXB	Park Royal	H43/33F	1977	Ex West Midlands Travel, 1990
HIL3073	Daimler Fleetline CRG6LXB	Willowbrook	H43/33F	1977	Ex Hewlett & Sutton, 1986
HIL3074	Daimler Fleetline CRG6LXB	Willowbrook	H43/33F	1977	Ex Hewlett & Sutton, 1986
HIL3477	Daimler Fleetline CRL6	Park Royal	H43/33F	1977	Ex West Midlands Travel, 1990
HIL3478	Daimler Fleetline CRL6	Park Royal	H43/33F	1977	Ex West Midlands Travel, 1990
HIL8670	Leyland Leopard PSU3E/4R	Duple Dominant II	C53F	1977	Ex PMT, 1992
IIL4005	Leyland Tiger TRCTL11/3R	Plaxton Paramount 3500	C50F	1983	Ex MacPherson, Coalville, 1992
GIL2163	Bova FHD12.280	Bova Futura	C49FT	1984	Ex Enterprise, Chatteris, 1993
LAT255	Van Hool T815H	Van Hool Alizée	C49FT	1985	Ex Lattimore, Markyate, 1992
B523CHD	DAF MB200DKVL600	Duple Caribbean 2	C49FT	1985	Ex Hollis Coaches, Sealand, 1993
H829AHS	Volvo B10M-60	Plaxton Paramount 3500 III	C53F	1991	Ex Parks, Hamilton, 1993
J18ERH	Mercedes-Benz 609D	Plaxton Beaver	C24F	1991	

Previous Registrations:

HIL3073	NFA16M	HIL3478	GOG530N	IIL4005	A509HVT
HIL3074	NFA19M	HIL3479	EOF278L	GIL2163	3927TR, A630FRM
HIL3477	GOG536N	HIL8670	KWG131W	LAT255	A514HBC

Livery: Blue and white

Roger Hill use their double-deck vehicles on school contracts in the Macclesfield area. Departing Tytherington High School is HIL3074, an East Lancashire bodied Daimler Fleetline unmistakeably new to Nottingham. *Graham Ashworth*

The North Midland Bus Handbook

ROYAL MAIL POST BUS

0750106 J25ECA	Leyland-DAF Sherpa	Post Office	M10	1991	Chester - Huxley
2750019 K985BUK	Leyland-DAF Sherpa	Post Office	M10	1993	Stafford - Adbaston
2750021 L711JFA	Leyland-DAF Sherpa	Post Office	M10	1993	Reserve
2750022 K297AOL	Leyland-DAF Sherpa	Post Office	M10	1993	Stafford - Adbaston
2750032 K630EYX	Leyland-DAF Sherpa	Post Office	M10	1993	Stafford - Adbaston
375 L	Leyland-DAF Sherpa	Post Office	M10	1994	On order for Leek
375 L	Leyland-DAF Sherpa	Post Office	M10	1994	On order for Rugeley

2750032 has recently returned from taking part in a relief food convoy to Bosnia.

Livery: Post Office Red

SELWYNS

Selwyn's Travel Ltd, Cavendish Farm Road, Runcorn, Cheshire, WA7 4LU

10	B163PRK	Mercedes-Benz L608D	Devon Conversions	C15F	1984	Ex Wincanton, London, 1988
11	D895SWM	Mercedes-Benz L307D	Whittaker	M12	1987	
13	D846RHS	Mercedes-Benz 609D	Devon Conversions	C19F	1987	
14	D845RHS	Mercedes-Benz 609D	Devon Conversions	C19F	1987	
15	E427ATT	Mercedes-Benz 609D	Devon Conversions	C19F	1987	
16	K3SEL	Mercedes-Benz 609D	Autobus Classique	C15F	1992	
20	ATV746T	Bedford YLQ	Plaxton Supreme III	C45F	1978	Ex Brumpton, Dunham, 1985
21	EDM900X	Bedford YMP	Plaxton Supreme V Express	C45F	1982	Ex Hanmer, Wrexham, 1988
22	E406LPR	Bedford YMP	Plaxton Paramount 3200 III	C35F	1988	Ex C&E, Hersham, 1991
23	F360MUT	Dennis Javelin 8.5SDL1903	Plaxton Paramount 3200 III	C35F	1988	Ex Davis, Minchinhampton, 1992
24	A672XFM	Auwaerter Neoplan N116	Auwaerter Jetliner	C49FT	1983	
25	D114LSE	Bedford YMP	Plaxton Paramount 3200 III	C35F	1987	Ex Jamieson, Cullivoe, 1993
26	SEL392	Volvo B10M-61	Van Hool Alizée	C53F	1985	Ex The Wright Company, Wrexham, 1988
27	D620YCX	DAF SB2300DHTD585	Plaxton Paramount 3500 III	C53F	1987	
28	E500CTU	DAF SB2305DHTD585	Plaxton Paramount 3500 III	C53F	1987	
29	E901EAY	Bedford YMP	Plaxton Paramount 3200 III	C43F	1987	
30	D34BRS	MCW Metroliner HR131/10	MCW	C36FT	1987	Ex Northern Bus, Anston, 1993
31	352STG	MCW Metroliner HR131/10	MCW	C26FT	1987	Ex Northern Bus, Anston, 1993
32	F724JTU	Volvo B10M-60	Plaxton Paramount 3500 III	C49FT	1989	
33	F725JTU	Volvo B10M-60	Plaxton Paramount 3500 III	C49FT	1989	
34	F399KTU	Volvo B10M-60	Plaxton Paramount 3500 III	C49FT	1989	
36	SEL853	Mercedes-Benz 0303/15RHD	Mercedes-Benz	C53F	1987	Ex Hirst, Holmfirth, 1990
37	SEL36	Mercedes-Benz 0303/15RHD	Mercedes-Benz	C53F	1987	Ex Hirst, Holmfirth, 1990
40	D50OWJ	MCW Metroliner HR131/9	MCW	C53F	1987	Ex Northern Bus, Anston, 1993
54	SEL73	Auwaerter Neoplan N122/3	Auwaerter Skyliner	CH55/18CT	1988	Ex International Leisure, Ratby, 1990
55	SEL133	Auwaerter Neoplan N122/3	Auwaerter Skyliner	CH57/20CT	1988	Ex International Leisure, Ratby, 1991
57	SEL23	Auwaerter Neoplan N122/3	Auwaerter Skyliner	CH57/20CT	1988	Ex International Leisure, Ratby, 1992

Previous Registrations:

352STG	D57XSS, 542GRT, D43BRS	SEL23	E475VWJ
A672XFM	A144RVL, SEL73	SEL36	D347CBC
D34BRS	D56XSS, TRS333	SEL73	E483YWJ
E500CTU	E314EVH, SEL36	SEL853	D346CBC
SEL133	F615CWJ	SEL392	B122DMA

Livery: White, green, orange and blue

The vehicles of Cheshire coach operator Selwyns of Runcorn are frequent visitors to the capital city. SEL392 a Van Hool-bodied Volvo B10M is seen unloading passengers outside the West Door of Westminster Abbey.
Colin Lloyd

SERVEVERSE

Serveverse Ltd, 11 Greenlee, Stoneydelph, Tamworth, Staffordshire.

MMB971P	Leyland National 1151/1R/SC		DP49F	1975	Ex Evans, Tregaron, 1992
JOX496P	Leyland National 11351/1R		B52F	1975	Ex Midland Red West, 1993
OOX820R	Leyland National 11351A/1R		DP45F	1976	Ex C & H, Fleetwood, 1992
YCD83T	Leyland National 11351A/2R		B44D	1978	Ex Thames Transit, 1992
YCD84T	Leyland National 11351A/2R		B44D	1978	Ex Thames Transit, 1992
D525NDA	Freight Rover Sherpa	Carlyle	B19F	1987	Ex Staffordian, Stafford, 1993
L321BNX	Mercedes-Benz 811D	Plaxton Beaver	B31F	1994	

Livery: Light green and White

Serveverse commenced operations on Birmingham local services in competition with West Midlands Travel in January 1992. The base is at Mile Oak and there are nine vehicles in the fleet. Typical of the six Leyland Nationals is JOX496P an example new to Midland Red. Some vehicles carry 'Serverse' as a fleetname. *Keith Grimes*

SHROPSHIRE EDUCATION

Shropshire County Council, Shirehall, Abbey Foregate, Shrewsbury, Shropshire, SY2 6ND

XDF7X	Ford R1114	Duple Dominant IV	C53F	1982	Ex Hand, Horsley, 1983
ETA978Y	Ford R1114	Duple Dominant IV	C53F	1983	Ex Devonways, Kingskerswell, 1983
GEX214Y	Ford R1115	Duple Dominant IV	C53F	1983	Ex Bird, Hunstanton, 1989
A653ANT	Ford R1114	Duple Dominant IV	C53F	1983	
B139HUJ	Freight Rover Sherpa	Freight Rover	M16	1984	
B341BBV	Ford R1115	Plaxton Paramount 3200 II	C53F	1985	Ex Stott, Oldham, 1991
G574BHP	Peugeot-Talbot Freeway	Talbot	B12DL	1989	Ex Peugeot-Talbot demonstrator, 1991
G971BHP	Peugeot-Talbot Freeway	Talbot	B12DL	1989	Ex Peugeot-Talbot demonstrator, 1991
H482ONT	Peugeot-Talbot Pullman	Talbot	B15F	1990	
H483ONT	Peugeot-Talbot Pullman	Talbot	B15F	1990	
H485ONT	Peugeot-Talbot Pullman	Talbot	B15F	1990	
H157EFK	Peugeot-Talbot Pullman	Talbot	B15F	1990	

Livery: White

Shropshire County Council operate vehicles mostly on school contracts, but also now operate on two tendered services in the county. Seen on school contract work is ETA978Y, a Duple Dominant IV-bodied Ford. The livery of all-white is relieved by the county coat of arms and the county name.
Bill Potter

STAFFORDIAN

Staffordian Travel Ltd, Greyfriars Coach Station, Greyfriars Way, Stafford,
Staffordshire, ST16 2SH

112	E986FFV	Iveco Turbo 35-10	Mellor	M12	1987	Ex PMT, 1992
124	H742VHS	Mercedes-Benz 609D	Scott	C24F	1990	Ex Kyle, Kelso, 1993
149	SUX260R	Ford R1114	Duple Dominant	C53F	1977	Ex Bennets, Gloucester, 1989
153	YRE465S	Ford R1114	Duple Dominant II	C53F	1978	Ex Greatrex, Stafford, 1985
154	GEH299T	Ford R1114	Duple Dominant II	C53F	1979	Ex Greatrex, Stafford, 1985
155	GEH300T	Ford R1114	Duple Dominant II	C53F	1979	Ex Greatrex, Stafford, 1985
158	XWX175S	Leyland Leopard PSU3E/4R	Duple Dominant II	C53F	1978	Ex O'Brien, Farnworth, 1987
161	NXR835	Volvo B10M-61	Berkhof Everest 365	C51F	1983	Ex Smith, Alcester, 1988
163	XSU978	Leyland Tiger TRCTL11/3R	Plaxton Paramount 3500	C49FT	1983	Ex Winn, Brompton, 1993
164	KLX443	Volvo B10M-61	Berkhof Everest 365	C51F	1983	Ex Smith, Alcester, 1988
165	MIB580	DAF MB200DKFL600	Duple Caribbean	C49F	1985	Ex Wallace Arnold, 1986
166	L300BVA	Volvo B10M-60	Jonckheere Deauville P599	C51FT	1993	

Previous Registrations:

MIB580	B583BCX		KLX443	JJN181Y
NXR835	JJN180Y		XSU978	BAJ635Y

Livery: Grey and red

Staffordian are associated with Happy Days and also work from Stafford sharing the same fleet number series. Photographed in Pitcher Bank in the town is PBO675R, showing off this operators livery on Plaxton Supreme bodywork. *Graham Ashworth*

STAR LINE

Arrow Line Travel Ltd, PO Box 32, Knutsford, Cheshire, WA16 6BD

MIB3957	Leyland Tiger TRCTL11/3R	Plaxton Paramount 3200	C53F	1983	Ex Bullock, Cheadle, 1989
F378UCP	Mercedes-Benz 609D	Reeve Burgess Beaver	B18F	1988	Ex Yorkshire Rider, 1990
H407BVR	Mercedes-Benz 609D	Reeve Burgess Beaver	B20F	1990	
H408BVR	Mercedes-Benz 709D	Reeve Burgess Beaver	B25F	1990	
H409BVR	Mercedes-Benz 709D	Reeve Burgess Beaver	B25F	1990	
H404BVR	Mercedes-Benz 814D	Carlyle	C29F	1991	
H415BVR	Mercedes-Benz 709D	Carlyle	B29F	1991	
J291NNB	Mercedes-Benz 709D	Carlyle	B29F	1991	
J292NNB	Mercedes-Benz 709D	Carlyle	B29F	1991	
J293NNB	Mercedes-Benz 709D	Carlyle	B29F	1991	
J295NNB	Mercedes-Benz 709D	Reeve Burgess Beaver	B25F	1992	
J296NNB	Mercedes-Benz 709D	Reeve Burgess Beaver	B25F	1992	
J297NNB	Mercedes-Benz 709D	Reeve Burgess Beaver	B25F	1992	
J298NNB	Mercedes-Benz 709D	Reeve Burgess Beaver	B25F	1992	
J299NNB	Mercedes-Benz 709D	Reeve Burgess Beaver	B25F	1992	
J648XHL	Dennis Dart 9.8SDL3004	Plaxton Pointer	B40F	1991	Ex Plaxton demonstrator, 1992
K876UDB	Mercedes-Benz 709D	Plaxton Beaver	B29F	1992	
K877UDB	Dennis Dart 9.8SDL3017	Plaxton Pointer	B40F	1992	
K878UDB	Mercedes-Benz 709D	Plaxton Beaver	B29F	1993	
K879UDB	Mercedes-Benz 709D	Plaxton Beaver	B29F	1993	
K880UDB	Mercedes-Benz 814D	Dormobile Routemaker	DP29F	1993	
K881UDB	Mercedes-Benz 709D	Plaxton Beaver	B29F	1992	
K882UDB	Mercedes-Benz 709D	Plaxton Beaver	B29F	1992	
K884UDB	Mercedes-Benz 709D	Plaxton Beaver	B29F	1993	
K887UDB	Mercedes-Benz 709D	Plaxton Beaver	B29F	1993	
K890UDB	Toyota Coaster HDB30R	Caetano Optimo II	C18F	1993	
K100SLT	Dennis Javelin 10SDA2119	Berkhof Excellence 1000 L	C32FT	1993	
K200SLT	Dennis Javelin 12SDA2117	Berkhof Excellence 1000 L	C51FT	1993	
L641DNA	Mercedes-Benz 709D	Plaxton Beaver	B29F	1993	
L642DNA	Mercedes-Benz 709D	Plaxton Beaver	B29F	1994	
L643DNA	Mercedes-Benz 709D	Plaxton Beaver	B29F	1993	
L644DNA	Mercedes-Benz 709D	Plaxton Beaver	B29F	1993	
L3SLT	Dennis Javelin 10SDA2119	Berkhof Excellence 1000 L	C41F	1993	
L4SLT	Toyota Coaster HDB30R	Caetano Optimo II	C18F	1994	
L5SLT	Toyota Coaster HDB30R	Caetano Optimo II	C18F	1994	
L8SLT	Dennis Javelin 12SDA2117	Berkhof Excellence 1000 L	C51F	1994	
L646DNA	Mercedes-Benz 709D	Dormobile Routemaker	B29F	1994	
L647DNA	Mercedes-Benz 709D	Plaxton Beaver	B29F	1994	
L651DNA	Dennis Dart 9SDL3017	Northern Counties	B40F	In build	
L652DNA	Dennis Dart 9SDL3017	Northern Counties	B40F	In build	
L653DNA	Dennis Dart 9SDL3017	Northern Counties	B40F	In build	

Previous Registrations:
MIB3957   DNB125Y

Livery: Blue, white and red.

Not to be over shadowed by the bus fleet, the coach fleet is also receiving considerable investment, standardising on the Berkhof-bodied Dennis Javelin. K200SLT, seen parked at Withington, Manchester, is being used to target the corporate and executive travel market, enhanced by the proximity to Manchester International Airport. *Graham Ashworth*

K882UDB is seen at Davenport Green on Star Line's commercial service from Knutsford through Wilmslow to Althrincham. Now the company's standard minibus it is a Mercedes-Benz 709D with Plaxton Beaver bodywork. The 27-seaters conform to GMPTE specification while the 29-seaters are for Cheshire Bus services. *Graham Ashworth*

STEVENSONS

Stevensons of Uttoxeter Ltd, The Garage, Spath, Uttoxeter, Staffordshire, ST14 5AE
Blue Triangle Coach & Bus Ltd, Crystal Coaches Ltd, Sealandair (Coaching) Ltd,
The Garage, Spath, Uttoxeter, Staffordshire, ST14 5AE

Hot Lane, Burslem; Wetmore Road, Burton-on-Trent; Power Station Road, Rugeley; Unit 11, London Street, Smethwick; Midland Road, Swadlincote; Ryder Close, Cadley Hill, Swadlincote; The Garage, Spath; Oak Road, West Bromwich; Tunnel Road, Hill Top, West Bromwich and Ashmore Lake Works, Willenhall.

1	HIJ3652	Volvo B10M-61	Plaxton Paramount 3500	C49FT	1984	Ex Bagnall, Swadlincote, 1989
2	82HBC	DAF MB200DKFL600	Plaxton Paramount 3200	C53F	1986	Ex Viking, Woodville, 1987
3	AJF405A	Volvo B58-56	Plaxton Supreme IV	C53F	1980	Ex Wallace Arnold, 1985
4	614WEH	Volvo B58-61	Plaxton P 3200 II (1986)	C53F	1976	Ex Coliseum, Southampton, 1985
5	AEH607A	Volvo B58-56	Plaxton Supreme IV Express	C53F	1981	Ex Mayor, Freckleton, 1985
6	PFA6W	Leyland Leopard PSU3E/4R	Plaxton Supreme IV	C53F	1981	
7	422AKN	Leyland Leopard PSU3E/4R	Plaxton Supreme III	C53F	1978	
8	AAX562A	Leyland Leopard PSU3E/4R	Plaxton Supreme III Express	C53F	1977	Ex Greater Manchester PTE, 1984
9	G417WFP	Bova FHD12.290	Bova Futura	C36FT	1990	Ex Boyden, Castle Donington, 1991
10	488BDN	Leyland Leopard PSU3C/4R	Plaxton Elite	DP53F	1975	Ex Selwyn, Runcorn, 1984
11	YSG339	Leyland Leopard PSU3C/4R	Plaxton Elite	C53F	1975	Ex Selwyn, Runcorn, 1984
12	AAL303A	Leyland Leopard PSU5D/4R	Plaxton P 3200 (1987)	C53F	1980	Ex Rhonda, 1992
13	AAL404A	Leyland Leopard PSU5D/4R	Plaxton P 3200 (1987)	C53F	1980	Ex Rhonda, 1992
14	LUY742	Volvo B10M-61	Plaxton Paramount 3500 III	C49FT	1987	Ex Sealandair, West Bromwich, 1991
15	VOI6874	Volvo B10M-61	Plaxton Paramount 3500 III	C53F	1983	Ex Bagnall, Swadlincote, 1989
16	SOA676S	Leyland Leopard PSU3E/4R	Plaxton Supreme III Express	C53F	1977	Ex Rhondda, 1993
17	WYR562	Leyland Leopard PSU3E/4R	Plaxton Supreme III Express	C53F	1978	Ex Greater Manchester PTE, 1984
18	479BOC	Leyland Leopard PSU3B/4R	Duple 320 (1987)	C53F	1973	Ex Blue Bus, Rugeley, 1985
19	468KPX	Volvo B10M-61	Van Hool Alizée	C48F	1982	Ex Cumberland, 1992
20	784RBF	Volvo B10M-61	Jonckheere Jubilee P50	C53F	1987	Ex Telling-Golden Miller, 1993
21	G21YVT	Volvo B10M-60	Van Hool Alizée	C49F	1989	
22	G122DRF	Volvo B10M-60	Van Hool Alizée	C53F	1990	
23	852YYC	Volvo B58-61	Plaxton Supreme IV	C49DL	1980	Ex Greater Manchester PTE, 1985
24	124YTW	Volvo B58-61	Plaxton Supreme IV	C53F	1980	Ex Greater Manchester PTE, 1985
25	G25YVT	Volvo B10M-60	Plaxton Paramount 3200 III	C53F	1989	
26	XOR841	Volvo B10M-61	Van Hool Alizée	C53F	1983	Ex Sealandair, West Bromwich, 1991
27	TOU962	Volvo B10M-61	Van Hool Alizée	C53F	1983	Ex Sealandair, West Bromwich, 1991
29	LFR532F	Leyland Titan PD3/11	MCW	H41/30R	1968	Ex Eastbourne, 1993
30	PAX466F	Leyland Titan PD3/4	Massey	L35/33RD	1968	Ex Rhymney Valley, 1982
31	J31SFA	Leyland Swift ST2R44C97A4	Wright Handy-bus	B39F	1992	
32	J32SFA	Leyland Swift ST2R44C97A4	Wright Handy-bus	B39F	1992	
33	H313WUA	Leyland Swift ST2R44C97A4	Reeve Burgess Harrier	DP39F	1991	Ex Pennine, Gargrave, 1992
34	J34SRF	Leyland Swift ST2R44C97A4	Wright Handy-bus	B39F	1992	

The oldest vehicle in the Stevenson fleet is 30, PAX466F. It is one of the very few remaining lowbridge double deckers in service anywhere in the country. The Massey body has a capacity of 68 on its Leyland PD3/4 chassis. It came from Rhymney Valley to Stevensons in 1982, and was re-engined with a Leyland 0600 unit in 1986.
Cliff Beeton

Stevensons 31, J31SFA, is the first of a batch of four Wright-bodied Leyland Swifts which were new in 1992. These vehicles are 39-seaters. This vehicle is allocated to Willenhall in the Black Country and is seen in Wolverhampton bus station prior to working to Stowlawn. *Mike Fowler*

No.38, F907PFH, is the oddest looking Leyland Swift in the Stevenson fleet. It was bodied by GC Smith of Long Whatton for the Gloucestershire County Council welfare fleet. Purchased in September 1992, it was converted by Stevensons to a 36-seat bus before entering service in July 1993. The photograph was taken in High Street, Burton when the vehicle was en route to Swadlincote. *David Stanier*

35	H314WUA	Leyland Swift ST2R44C97A4	Reeve Burgess Harrier	DP39F	1991	Ex Pennine, Gargrave, 1992
36	J36SRF	Leyland Swift ST2R44C97A4	Wright Handy-bus	B39F	1992	
37	G616WGS	Leyland Swift LBM6T/2RA	Reeve Burgess Harrier	B39F	1989	Ex Chambers, Stevenage, 1992
38	F907PFH	Leyland Swift LBM6T/2RA	G C Smith Whippet	B36F	1988	Ex Gloucs County Council, 1993
39	G727RGA	Leyland Swift LBM6T/2RA	Reeve Burgess Harrier	B39F	1990	Ex Kelvin Central, 1993
40	J556GTP	Dennis Dart 9SDL3002	Wadham Stringer Portsdown	B35F	1991	Ex Irwell Valley, Boothstown, 1992
41	G141GOL	Dennis Dart 9SDL3002	Duple Dartline	B36F	1990	Ex Star Line, Knutsford, 1992
42	H851NOC	Dennis Dart 9.8SDL3004	Carlyle Dartline	B43F	1991	Ex Thanet Bus, Ramsgate, 1992
43	L43MEH	MAN 11.190	Optare Vecta	B41F	1994	
44	JHE189W	MCW Metrobus DR104/6	MCW	H46/31F	1981	Ex South Yorkshire, 1990
45	H192JNF	Dennis Dart 9SDL3002	Wadham Stringer Portsdown	B35F	1990	Ex Jim Stones, Glazebury, 1993
46	JHE145W	MCW Metrobus DR104/6	MCW	H46/31F	1981	Ex South Yorkshire, 1990
47	JHE192W	MCW Metrobus DR104/6	MCW	H46/31F	1981	Ex South Yorkshire, 1990
48	BOK68V	MCW Metrobus DR102/12	MCW	H43/30F	1980	Ex West Midlands Travel, 1990
49	GOG223W	MCW Metrobus DR102/18	MCW	H43/30F	1981	Ex West Midlands Travel, 1990
50	GOG272W	MCW Metrobus DR102/18	MCW	H43/30F	1981	Ex West Midlands Travel, 1990

51-56 MCW Metrobus DR102/22 MCW H43/30F 1981 Ex West Midlands Travel, 1990

51	KJW296W	53	KJW305W	54	KJW306W	55	KJW310W	56	KJW322W
52	KJW301W						

57	JHE193W	MCW Metrobus DR104/6	MCW	H46/31F	1981	Ex South Yorkshire, 1990
58	JHE137W	MCW Metrobus DR104/6	MCW	H46/31F	1981	Ex South Yorkshire, 1990
59	JHE138W	MCW Metrobus DR104/6	MCW	H46/31F	1981	Ex South Yorkshire, 1990
60	D401MHS	Leyland Lynx LX5636LXCTFR1	Leyland Lynx	B47F	1986	Ex Kelvin Central, 1991
61	F61PRE	Leyland Lynx LX112L10ZR1R	Leyland Lynx	B48F	1989	
62	J162REH	Leyland Swift ST2R44C97A4	Wadham Stringer Vanguard II	B39F	1991	

Stevenson 61, F61PRE, is a Leyland Lynx new in 1989 as a 51-seater, but since converted to 49. Although not the preserve of the Leyland Lynx, the 112 service from Burton on Trent to Birmingham is often worked by one of them. *David Stanier*

Above: **November 1992 saw the arrival of Dennis Dart 40, J556GTP, from Irwell Valley of Boothstown. This has a Wadham Stringer Portsdown body that is more orthodox in its appearance than the Carlyle version seen** *below*. **Allocated to Rugeley this vehicle may be seen working Service 823 thence to Lichfield. The Duple Dartline design has now become well known, and continues in a modified form by Marshalls, to whom the design rights passed from Carlyle. G141GOL is fleet number 41 and was originally a Carlyle demonstrator. This particular vehicle was started by Duple before passing to Carlyle, though it was not registered until May 1990.** *David Stanier*

63	MFR126P	Leyland Leopard PSU4C/2R	Alexander AYS	B45F	1976	Ex Lancaster, 1984
64	MFR125P	Leyland Leopard PSU4C/2R	Alexander AYS	B45F	1976	Ex Lancaster, 1984
65	MFR41P	Leyland Leopard PSU4C/2R	Alexander AY	B45F	1976	Ex Lancaster, 1982
66	H166MFA	Leyland Swift ST2R44C97A4	Wadham Stringer Vanguard II B39F		1991	
67	F956XCK	Leyland Swift LBM6N/2RAO	Wadham Stringer Vanguard II B39F		1989	Ex Jim Stones, Glazebury, 1991
68	G98VMM	Leyland Swift LBM6T/2RA	Wadham Stringer Vanguard II B39F		1989	Ex Green, Kirkintilloch, 1991
69	J169REH	Leyland Swift ST2R44C97A4	Wadham Stringer Vanguard II B39F		1991	
70	KJW318W	MCW Metrobus DR102/22	MCW	H43/30F	1981	Ex West Midlands Travel, 1990
71	KJW320W	MCW Metrobus DR102/22	MCW	H43/30F	1981	Ex West Midlands Travel, 1990
72	E72KBF	Leyland Lynx LX112L10ZR1	Leyland Lynx	B51F	1988	
73	UWW512X	MCW Metrobus DR101/15	Alexander RH	H43/32F	1982	Ex West Yorkshire PTE, 1987
74	UWW513X	MCW Metrobus DR101/15	Alexander RH	H43/32F	1982	Ex West Yorkshire PTE, 1987
75	UWW515X	MCW Metrobus DR101/15	Alexander RH	H43/32F	1982	Ex West Yorkshire PTE, 1987
76	UWW517X	MCW Metrobus DR101/15	Alexander RH	H43/32F	1982	Ex West Yorkshire PTE, 1987
77	GBU3V	MCW Metrobus DR101/6	MCW	H43/30F	1979	Ex Greater Manchester, 1987
78	GBU7V	MCW Metrobus DR101/6	MCW	H43/30F	1979	Ex Greater Manchester, 1987
79	BSN878V	MCW Metrobus DR102/5	MCW	H45/30F	1979	Ex Enterprise & Silver Dawn, 1988
80	TOJ592S	MCW Metrobus DR101/2	MCW	H43/30F	1977	Ex MCW demonstrator, 1991
81	F181YDA	MCW Metrobus DR104/64	MCW	H43/30F	1988	Ex MCW demonstrator, 1989
82	BOK72V	MCW Metrobus DR102/12	MCW	H43/30F	1980	Ex West Midlands Travel, 1989
83	BOK75V	MCW Metrobus DR102/12	MCW	H43/30F	1980	Ex West Midlands Travel, 1989
86	JWF490W	MCW Metrobus DR102/13	MCW	H46/30F	1980	Ex South Yorkshire, 1988
87	JWF493W	MCW Metrobus DR102/13	MCW	H46/30F	1980	Ex South Yorkshire, 1988
88	JWF494W	MCW Metrobus DR102/13	MCW	H46/30F	1980	Ex South Yorkshire, 1988
89	D676MHS	MCW Metrobus DR102/52	Alexander RL	DPH45/33F	1986	Ex Kelvin Central, 1994
90	D678MHS	MCW Metrobus DR102/52	Alexander RL	DPH45/33F	1986	Ex Kelvin Central, 1994
91	D680MHS	MCW Metrobus DR102/52	Alexander RL	DPH45/33F	1986	Ex Kelvin Central, 1994
92	D682MHS	MCW Metrobus DR102/52	Alexander RL	DPH45/33F	1986	Ex Kelvin Central, 1994
93	D683MHS	MCW Metrobus DR102/52	Alexander RL	DPH45/33F	1986	Ex Kelvin Central, 1994
94	L94HRF	DAF DB250RS200505	Optare Spectra	H48/29F	1993	
95	L95HRF	DAF DB250RS200505	Optare Spectra	H48/29F	1993	
96	F96PRE	Leyland Olympian ONCL10/1RZ	Alexander RL	H47/32F	1988	
97	F97PRE	Leyland Olympian ONCL10/1RZ	Alexander RL	H47/32F	1988	
99	Q246FVT	Leyland Olympian B45-6LXB	Eastern Coach Works	H43/30F	1979	Ex Leyland development, 1983
100	L100SBS	Mercedes-Benz Cityranger 0405	Wright Endurance	B51F	1993	
101	L	Mercedes-Benz 1416	Wright	B	On order	
102	L102MEH	Volvo B6	Plaxton Pointer	B F	1994	
104	PCW946	Leyland Leopard PSU3E/4R	Plaxton Supreme III Express C53F		1977	Ex Thomas, Stockport, 1985
105	E829AWA	Leyland TRCTL11/2RP	Plaxton Derwent	B54F	1988	Ex Liverline, Liverpool, 1993

Opposite, top: **The only Mercedes-Benz 0405 service bus in the West Midlands area is Stevensons' Wright-bodied example numbered 100, L100SBS. This entered service with Stevensons in August 1993. Note the Select registration used on this vehicle.** *Phillip Stephenson*

Opposite, bottom: **G109YRE is one of three Scania K93 in the fleet and one of a pair with Alexander bodywork. It is photographed at Burton on Trent.** *Tony Wilson*

Twelve MCW Metrobuses were purchased by Stevensons from West Midlands Travel in 1990. They were then ten or eleven years old, but should be capable of many more years of service. No.82, BOK72V, is a MCW DR102/12 model and is awaiting service on a Burton on Trent to Swadlincote run. *David Stanier*

The only Leyland Tiger in the fleet is 105, E829AWA, a Plaxton Derwent 54-seat bus, new in 1988. This was one of the 1993 acquisitions, and came from Liverline in Liverpool. It is seen working another important Stevensons Route - 118 from Burton on Trent to Leicester. *David Stanier*

Far right: The newest double deckers in the Stevensons fleet are a pair of Optare Spectras based on the DAF DB250 underframe. These vehicles are 77 seaters, at present allocated to Rugeley for working the 112 Burton-Birmingham service. No.95, L95HRF, is photographed at the Burton on Trent terminus of the route shortly after delivery. *David Stanier*

Right: Heading south to Birmingham is Leyland Olympian 96, F96PRE. Fitted with the R-type body by Aleanders it was one of a pair delivered in 1988. *Bill Potter*

Below: Stevensons 99, Q246FVT, has been in the fleet for over ten years. Originally a Leyland development vehicle, it was the original Olympian prototype, then called the B45. When purchased by Stevensons in June 1983, it was incomplete and unlike a demonstator had never been registered. The Eastern Coach Works-constructed shell was fitted out by Stevensons, though the vehicle did not enter regular service until January 1985. *David Stanier*

106	H408YMA	Leyland Lynx LX2R11C15Z4R	Leyland Lynx	B49F	1990	Ex The Wright Company, 1994
107	F170DET	Scania K93CRB	Plaxton Derwent	B57F	1989	Ex Capital Citybus, 1993
108	F258GWJ	Leyland Lynx LX112L10ZR1R	Leyland Lynx	B51F	1989	Ex The Wright, Company, 1993
109	G109YRE	Scania K93CRB	Alexander PS	B51F	1989	
110	F110SRF	Scania K93CRB	Alexander PS	B51F	1989	
111	VAJ785S	Leyland Leopard PSU3E/4R	Willowbrook Warrior (1990)	B48F	1977	Ex South Lancs Transport, 1994
112	GNL838N	Leyland Leopard PSU3B/4R	Alexander AY	DP49F	1975	Ex Chase, Chasetown, 1993
113	YSF85S	Leyland Leopard PSU3E/4R	Alexander AYS	B53F	1977	Ex Fife Scottish, 1992
114	BSD846T	Seddon Pennine 7	Alexander AY	B53F	1979	Ex Clydeside Scottish, 1988
115	YSF86S	Leyland Leopard PSU3E/4R	Alexander AYS	B53F	1977	Ex Fife Scottish, 1992
116	YSF93S	Leyland Leopard PSU3E/4R	Alexander AYS	B53F	1977	Ex Fife Scottish, 1992
117	F155DKU	Leyland Swift LBM6T/2RA	Reeve Burgess Harrier	B39F	1989	Ex K-Line, Kirkburton, 1993
118	GNL841N	Leyland Leopard PSU3C/4R	Alexander AY	B62F	1975	Ex Globe, Barnsley, 1991
119	VSX762R	Seddon Pennine 7	Alexander AY	B45F	1977	Ex Midland Scottish, 1990
120	GMS295S	Leyland Leopard PSU3E/4R	Alexander AY	B53F	1978	Ex Henley's, Abertillery, 1991
121	E990NMK	Leyland Swift LBM6T/2RS	Wadham Stringer Vanguard II	B37F	1988	Ex Armchair, Brentford, 1993
122	E992NMK	Leyland Swift LBM6T/2RS	Wadham Stringer Vanguard II	B37F	1988	Ex Armchair, Brentford, 1993
123	E993NMK	Leyland Swift LBM6T/2RS	Wadham Stringer Vanguard II	B37F	1988	Ex Armchair, Brentford, 1993
124	MFR18P	Leyland Leopard PSU3C/2R	Alexander AY	B53F	1976	Ex Lancaster, 1984
126	YSG652W	Seddon Pennine 7	Alexander AYS	B53F	1980	Ex Kelvin Central, 1989
127	F77ERJ	Mercedes-Benz 609D	Reeve Burgess Beaver	B27F	1988	Ex Star Line, Knutsford, 1991
128	D133NUS	Mercedes-Benz L608D	Alexander	B21F	1986	Ex Kelvin Central, 1992
129	D135NUS	Mercedes-Benz L608D	Alexander	B21F	1986	Ex Kelvin Central, 1992
130	D141NUS	Mercedes-Benz L608D	Alexander	B21F	1986	Ex Kelvin Central, 1992
131	K131XRE	Mercedes-Benz 709D	Dormobile	B29F	1992	
132	K132XRE	Mercedes-Benz 709D	Dormobile	B29F	1992	
133	J480XHL	Mercedes-Benz 709D	Alexander AM	DP25F	1991	Ex Mercedes-Benz demonstrator, 1993
134	F822GDT	Mercedes-Benz 811D	Reeve Burgess Beaver	C25F	1989	Ex Gordon, Rotherham, 1993
135	G807FJX	Mercedes-Benz 811D	PMT Ami	C33F	1990	Ex Traject, Halifax, 1993
136	K136ARE	Mercedes-Benz 709D	Wright	B29F	1992	
137	K137ARE	Mercedes-Benz 709D	Wright	B29F	1992	
138	K138BRF	Mercedes-Benz 811D	Dormobile Routemaker	B31F	1993	
139	K139BRF	Mercedes-Benz 811D	Dormobile Routemaker	B31F	1993	
140	K140BFA	Mercedes-Benz 811D	Dormobile Routemaker	B31F	1993	
141	K141BFA	Mercedes-Benz 811D	Dormobile Routemaker	B31F	1993	
142	K142BFA	Mercedes-Benz 811D	Dormobile Routemaker	B31F	1993	
143	J143SRF	Mercedes-Benz 709D	Wright	B29F	1992	
144	IDZ8561	Mercedes-Benz 811D	Wright	B26F	1990	Ex Wright demonstrator, 1992
146	E219SOL	MCW MetroRider MF150/37	MCW	DP25F	1987	Ex North Bedfordshire HA, 1991
147	K947BRE	Mercedes-Benz 709D	Dormobile Routemaker	B29F	1993	
148	K148BRF	Mercedes-Benz 709D	Dormobile Routemaker	B29F	1993	
150	K150BRF	Mercedes-Benz 709D	Wright	B27F	1992	
151	J151WEH	Mercedes-Benz 709D	Dormobile Routemaker	B29F	1992	
152	G702NGR	Mercedes-Benz 811D	Scott	C25F	1990	Ex Rush, Newcastle, 1993
154	K154BRF	Mercedes-Benz 709D	Dormobile Routemaker	B29F	1993	
155	K155CRE	Mercedes-Benz 709D	Dormobile Routemaker	B27F	1993	
156	K156BRF	Mercedes-Benz 709D	Dormobile Routemaker	B27F	1993	
157	K157BRF	Mercedes-Benz 709D	Dormobile Routemaker	B27F	1993	
158	K158BRF	Mercedes-Benz 709D	Dormobile Routemaker	B27F	1993	
159	E564YBU	Mercedes-Benz 709D	Reeve Burgess Beaver	B25F	1988	Ex Star Line, Knutsford, 1990
160	G160YRE	Mercedes-Benz 709D	LHE	B29F	1989	
161	G161YRE	Mercedes-Benz 709D	LHE	B29F	1989	
162	G162YRE	Mercedes-Benz 709D	LHE	B29F	1989	
163	G163YRE	Mercedes-Benz 709D	LHE	B29F	1989	

164-173

				Mercedes-Benz 709D	LHE			B29F	1990	

164	G164YRE	166	G166YRE	168	G168YRE	170	G170YRE	172	G172YRE
165	G165YRE	167	G167YRE	169	G169YRE	171	G171YRE	173	G173YRE

174	G174YRE	Mercedes-Benz 811D	Carlyle	B33F	1990	
175	G175DRF	Mercedes-Benz 811D	LHE	B33F	1990	
176	H176JVT	Mercedes-Benz 811D	Wright	B29F	1990	
177	H177JVT	Mercedes-Benz 811D	Wright	B29F	1990	
178	C78WRE	Mercedes-Benz L608D	PMT Hanbridge	DP19F	1986	
179	A343ASF	Mercedes-Benz L608D	Stevenson	B21F	1983	Ex Scottish Spastics, 1988
180	G301RJA	Mercedes-Benz 709D	Reeve Burgess Beaver	DP25F	1990	Ex Star Line, Knutsford, 1993
181	D176LNA	Mercedes-Benz 609D	Made-to-Measure	B25F	1986	Ex Marriott, Clayworth, 1988
182	D906MVU	Mercedes-Benz 609D	Made-to-Measure	B27F	1987	
183	G183DRF	Mercedes-Benz 709D	LHE	B29F	1990	
184	G184DRF	Mercedes-Benz 709D	LHE	B29F	1990	
185	F185PRE	Mercedes-Benz 709D	Robin Hood	B29F	1988	

There are now three Seddon Pennine 7s with Alexander bodywork remaining in service from batches of vehicles purchased from Kelvin Central, Midland and Clydeside Scottish in 1988 and 1989. No.119, VSX762R, is allocated to Swadlincote and was photographed awaiting departure in Burton on Trent.
David Stanier

Mercedes-Benz 709D models are the mainstay of Stevensons midibus fleet. Several different makes of body are fitted to this chassis. The one illustrated is 136, K136ARE, and has Wright bodywork.
David Stanier

In addition to Mercedes-Benz 709Ds, there are larger Mercedes-Benz 811Ds and 814Ds in the fleet. No.175, G175DRF, shown here has LHE 33-seat bodywork fitted to 811D a chassis cowl. Stevensons operate tendered services for several authorities. When photographed 175 was showing its Staffordshire bus sign to indicate this.
David Stanier

115

186	F186PRE	Mercedes-Benz 709D	Reeve Burgess Beaver	B25F	1988	
187	F187REH	Mercedes-Benz 609D	Whittaker Europa	B20F	1988	
188	F188REH	Mercedes-Benz 609D	PMT	B21F	1988	
189	F189RRF	Mercedes-Benz 709D	Robin Hood	B29F	1988	
190	F190RRF	Mercedes-Benz 709D	Robin Hood	B29F	1988	
191	F191SRF	Mercedes-Benz 709D	Robin Hood	B29F	1989	
192	F192VFA	Mercedes-Benz 709D	Robin Hood	B29F	1989	
193	F326PPO	Mercedes-Benz 709D	Robin Hood	B29F	1989	Ex Robin Hood demonstrator, 1989
194	B882HSX	Mercedes-Benz L608D	Stevenson	B21F	1984	Ex Scottish C for Spastics, 1989
195	F272OPX	Mercedes-Benz 811D	Robin Hood	DP29F	1988	Ex Robin Hood demonstrator, 1990
196	H196JVT	Mercedes-Benz 814D	Wright	B33F	1990	
197	H197JVT	Mercedes-Benz 814D	Wright	B33F	1990	
198	H198JVT	Mercedes-Benz 814D	Wright	B33F	1990	
199	H199KEH	Mercedes-Benz 814D	Phoenix	DP31F	1990	
200	565LON	MCW MetroRider MF154/10	MCW	C29F	1989	Ex PMT, 1991

201-207

Mercedes-Benz 814D   Wright   B31F*   1991   *201/2 are B33F

| 201 | H201LRF | 203 | J203REH | 205 | J205REH | 206 | J206REH | 207 | J207REH |
| 202 | H202LRF | 204 | J204REH | | | | | | |

| 208 | J208SRF | Mercedes-Benz 709D | Wright | B27F | 1992 | |
| 209 | J209SRF | Mercedes-Benz 709D | Wright | B27F | 1992 | |

210-221

Ford Transit 190D   Carlyle   B20F*   1985-86   Ex City of Oxford, 1991
*211/9 are B18F

210	B730YUD	213	B733YUD	215	B875EOM	218	B738YUD	220	C726JJO
211	B731YUD	214	B734YUD	217	B737YUD	219	C725JJO	221	C727JJO
212	B732YUD								

216	C539TJF	Ford Transit 190D	Rootes	B16F	1986	Ex Midland Fox, 1987
222	H880NFS	Mercedes-Benz 709D	PMT Ami	B29F	1991	Ex Gold Circle, Airdrie, 1994
223	C802SDY	Mercedes-Benz L608D	Alexander	B20F	1986	Ex Rainworth Travel, 1993
224	C823SDY	Mercedes-Benz L608D	Alexander	B20F	1986	Ex East Midland, 1993
225	C822SDY	Mercedes-Benz L608D	Alexander	B20F	1986	Ex East Midland, 1993

226-233

Mercedes-Benz 709D   Dormobile Routemaker   B27F*   1993   *226-8 are B29F

| 226 | L226JFA | 228 | L228HRF | 230 | L230HRF | 232 | L232HRF | 233 | L233HRF |
| 227 | L227HRF | 229 | L229HRF | 231 | L231HRF | | | | |

234	G142GOL	Mercedes-Benz 709D	Carlyle	B29F	1990	Ex Kentish Bus, 1993
235	G143GOL	Mercedes-Benz 709D	Carlyle	B29F	1990	Ex Kentish Bus, 1993
236	PFK174W	Ford R1114	Plaxton Supreme IV	C53F	1980	Ex Sealandair, West Bromwich, 1991
237	VFK660X	Ford R1114	Plaxton Supreme IV	C53F	1981	Ex Sealandair, West Bromwich, 1991
245	F985EDS	Mercedes Benz 811D	Alexander AM	DP33F	1989	Rhondda, 1994
246	803HOM	Volvo B58-61	Plaxton Supreme IV	C57F	1980	Ex Collett, West Bromwich, 1991
247	PSV323	Volvo B58-61	Plaxton Supreme IV	C57F	1980	Ex Classic, Wombourne, 1991
248	G65SNN	Mercedes-Benz 709D	Carlyle	DP29F	1990	Ex Skills, Nottingham, 1994
249	F836BCW	Mercedes-Benz 811D	Reeve Burgess Beaver	B33F	1989	Ex Powercraft, Blackburn, 1994
250	F835BCW	Mercedes-Benz 811D	Reeve Burgess Beaver	B33F	1989	Ex Powercraft, Blackburn, 1994
251	D71WTO	MCW MetroRider MF150/19	MCW	B23F	1987	Ex East Midland, 1993
252	D72WTO	MCW MetroRider MF150/20	MCW	B23F	1987	Ex East Midland, 1993
253	L253NFA	Mercedes-Benz		B F	On order	
254	L254NFA	Mercedes-Benz		B F	On order	
255	L255NFA	Mercedes-Benz		B F	On order	
256	HXI3006	Leyland Lynx LX5636LXCTFR	Alexander N	B49F	1985	Ex Citybus, Belfast, 1992
257	HXI3007	Leyland Lynx LX5636LXBFR	Alexander N	B49F	1986	Ex Citybus, Belfast, 1992
258	HXI3008	Leyland Lynx LX5636LXBFR	Alexander N	B49F	1986	Ex Citybus, Belfast, 1992
259	HXI3009	Leyland Lynx LX5636LXBFR	Alexander N	B49F	1986	Ex Citybus, Belfast, 1992
260	HXI3010	Leyland Lynx LX563TL11FR	Alexander N	B49F	1986	Ex Citybus, Belfast, 1992
261	HXI3011	Leyland Lynx LX563TL11FR	Alexander N	B53F	1986	Ex Citybus, Belfast, 1992
262	HXI3012	Leyland Lynx LX563TL11FR	Alexander N	B53F	1986	Ex Citybus, Belfast, 1992
263	E801UDT	MCW MetroRider MF150/15	MCW	B23F	1987	Ex East Midland, 1993
264	E802UDT	MCW MetroRider MF150/15	MCW	B23F	1987	Ex East Midland, 1993
265	E803UDT	MCW MetroRider MF150/15	MCW	B23F	1987	Ex East Midland, 1993
266	E804UDT	MCW MetroRider MF150/15	MCW	B23F	1987	Ex East Midland, 1993
267	E805UDT	MCW MetroRider MF150/15	MCW	B23F	1987	Ex East Midland, 1993
268	E806UDT	MCW MetroRider MF150/15	MCW	B23F	1987	Ex East Midland, 1993
269	E807UDT	MCW MetroRider MF150/15	MCW	B23F	1987	Ex East Midland, 1993

270-279   Ford Transit 190D   Carlyle   B20F*   1986   Ex Yorkshire Rider, 1992
*273-5/9 are B18F

270	C83AUB	272	C89AUB	274	C92AUB	276	C97AUB	278	D521HNW
271	C85AUB	273	C91AUB	275	C94AUB	277	C100AUB	279	D526HNW

280	E223PWY	MCW MetroRider MF150/34	MCW	DP23F	1987	Ex Yorkshire Rider, 1992
281	E232PWY	MCW MetroRider MF150/41	MCW	B23F	1987	Ex Yorkshire Rider, 1992
282	E222PWY	MCW MetroRider MF150/34	MCW	DP23F	1987	Ex Yorkshire Rider, 1992
283	E220PWY	MCW MetroRider MF150/34	MCW	DP23F	1987	Ex Yorkshire Rider, 1992
284	E224PWY	MCW MetroRider MF150/34	MCW	DP23F	1987	Ex Yorkshire Rider, 1992
285	E808UDT	MCW MetroRider MF150/15	MCW	B23F	1987	Ex East Midland, 1993
286	E809UDT	MCW MetroRider MF150/15	MCW	B23F	1987	Ex East Midland, 1993
287	E810UDT	MCW MetroRider MF150/15	MCW	B23F	1987	Ex East Midland, 1993
288	E811UDT	MCW MetroRider MF150/15	MCW	B23F	1987	Ex East Midland, 1993
289	E812UDT	MCW MetroRider MF150/15	MCW	B23F	1987	Ex East Midland, 1993
290	E604VKC	MCW MetroRider MF150/40	MCW	B23F	1987	Ex East Midland, 1993
291	E647DCK	Renault-Dodge S46	Dormobile Routemaker	B25F	1987	Ex Fife Scottish, 1992
292	E642DCK	Renault-Dodge S46	Dormobile Routemaker	B25F	1987	Ex Fife Scottish, 1992
300	L300SBS	Dennis Dart	Plaxton Pointer	B	On order	
301	L301NFA	Dennis Dart	Plaxton Pointer	B	On order	
302	L302NFA	Dennis Dart	Plaxton Pointer	B	On order	
303	L303NFA	Dennis Dart	Plaxton Pointer	B	On order	
304	L304NFA	Dennis Dart	Plaxton Pointer	B	On order	
305	L305NFA	Dennis Dart	Plaxton Pointer	B	On order	
350	TPD178M	Leyland National 1051/1R/0402		B41F	1973	Ex Blue Triangle, Rainham, 1994
351	MEX772W	Leyland National 11351A/1R		B52F	1976	Ex Evag Cannon, Bolton, 1994
352	KOM797P	Leyland National 11351A/2R		B46F	1976	Ex Evag Cannon, Bolton, 1994
353	THX126S	Leyland National 10351A/2R		B34F	1977	Ex Evag Cannon, Bolton, 1994

Previous Registrations:

124YTW	DEN247W	AAL404A	BUH222V	HXI3011	From new	
422AKN	XRE305S	AAX562A	OTD828R	HXI3012	From new	
468KPX	VRR447, UHH575X	AEH607A	MNT596W	IDZ8561	From new	
479BOC	AJA360L	AJF405A	LUA255V	LUY742	E562UHS	
488BDN	LMA60P	H192JNF	H1JYM	PCW946	TSJ678S	
565LON	F114UEH	HIJ3652	A703OWY	PSV323	HTV17V	
614WEH	LOT777R	HXI3006	From new	TOU962	MSU573Y	
784RBF	D319VVV	HXI3007	From new	VOI6874	YNN29Y	
803HOM	MDS231V	HXI3008	From new	WYR562	TWH687T	
82HBC	JGL53, DFP707Y	HXI3009	From new	XOR841	MHS665Y	
852YYC	DEN246W	HXI3010	From new	YSG339	LMA61P	
AAL303A	BUH226V					

Livery: Yellow and black; Sealandair - Maroon/pink; Victoria travel - Maroon/pink; Viking Coaches - two-tone grey.

Also on order are five Dennis Dart/Wright Handy-Bus. Fleet numbers are not yet allocated.

Seven Alexander- bodied Leyland Lynx were purchased from Citybus of Belfast in 1992. Now numbered 256 in the Stevensons fleet this vehicle, HXI3006, was one of the development Leyland Lynx chassis, and was originally a 37-seater vehicle, though Stevensons have fitted 53 seats. The vehicle is Gardner powered. For once the Irish registration is not a private mark, but was the one originally allocated to the vehicle when in service in Northern Ireland.
David Stanier

TONYS TRAVEL

A & M Lacking, 8 Eden Avenue, Wharton, Winsford, Cheshire.

H552WMB	Leyland DAF 400	Leyland DAF	M16	1991
K269JDM	Leyland DAF 400	Van Tech	M16	1992

Livery: Red

WALKER OF ANDERTON

G E & M V Walker, Malvern House, Old Road, Anderton, Northwich, Cheshire, CW9 6AG

MTU628H	Ford R226	Plaxton Elite	C53F	1969	
PRR106L	Bristol VRT/SL/6G	Eastern Coach Works	H39/31F	1972	Ex Crosville Wales, 1987
PRR108L	Bristol VRT/SL/6G	Eastern Coach Works	H39/31F	1972	Ex Crosville Wales, 1987
PRR110L	Bristol VRT/SL/6G	Eastern Coach Works	H39/31F	1972	Ex Crosville Wales, 1989
RUK522L	Ford R226	Plaxton Elite III	C53F	1973	Ex National Travel Midlands, 1978
VTB591L	Ford R226	Duple Dominant	C53F	1973	Ex Cosgrove, Preston, 1976
RAX826M	Ford R1014	Duple Dominant	C45F	1973	Ex R I Davies, Tredegar, 1975
XRR129M	Bristol VRT/SL/6G	Eastern Coach Works	H39/31F	1973	Ex East Midland, 1989
XRR132M	Bristol VRT/SL/6G	Eastern Coach Works	H39/31F	1973	Ex East Midland, 1989
XRR133M	Bristol VRT/SL/6G	Eastern Coach Works	H39/31F	1973	Ex East Midland, 1989
SAX632N	Ford R192	Duple Dominant	C45F	1974	Ex R I Davies, Tredegar, 1975
CJO468R	Bristol VRT/SL3/6LXB	Eastern Coach Works	H43/31F	1977	Ex Midland Red North, 1993
UMB976R	Ford R1114	Plaxton Supreme III	C53F	1977	
UUM500R	Ford R1114	Plaxton Supreme III	C53F	1977	
PFM508V	Ford R1114	Duple Dominant II	C53F	1979	
296HFM	Ford R1114	Plaxton Supreme IV	C53F	1979	
PUP565T	Ford R1114	Duple Dominant II	C53F	1979	Ex Bleanch, Hetton-le-Hole, 1981
EYK512V	Volvo B58-61	Plaxton Supreme IV	C49FT	1980	Ex Robin Hood, Rudyard, 1989
JLS457V	Volvo B58-61	Plaxton Supreme IV	C55F	1980	Ex Shearings, 1989
UTF119	Volvo B58-61	Plaxton Supreme IV	C57F	1980	Ex Wickson, Clayhanger, 1991
HOI7544	Volvo B58-56	Plaxton Supreme IV	C53F	1980	Ex Wickson, Clayhanger, 1991
152ENM	Volvo B58-61	Plaxton Supreme IV	C53F	1980	Ex Ingleby, Fulford, 19..
ASV237	Volvo B10M-61	Plaxton Supreme IV	C50F	1980	Ex Niddrie, Middlewich, 1989
NEK239W	Ford R1114	Duple Dominant IV	C53F	1981	Ex Lightfoot, Winsford, 1984
ACA507A	Volvo B58-61	Plaxton Supreme IV	C53F	1981	Ex WHM, Brentwood, 1988

PRR112L is a Bristol VRT new to East Midlands and is one of several double deck buses now used by Walkers on their school contract work. The current fleet of VRTs replaced several former SBG Alexander bodied Fleetlines and three Leyland Atlanteans from Blackburn.
Graham Ashworth

JHF826	Volvo B58-56	Plaxton Supreme IV	C53F	1981	Ex Woodstones, Kidderminster, 1988
ACA194A	Volvo B58-56	Plaxton Supreme IV	C53F	1981	Ex Cosgrove, Preston, 1989
PMB287Y	Ford R1114	Duple Dominant IV	C53F	1982	
PMB294Y	Ford R1114	Duple Dominant IV	C53F	1982	
DLG932X	Mercedes-Benz L508D	Whittaker	M16	1982	
CVU514Y	Ford Transit 190	Dixon Lomas	M12	1982	
505BRM	Volvo B10M-61	Duple Laser	C51F	1983	Ex Stewart, Dalmuir, 1985
A864KNA	Ford Transit 190	Dixon Lomas	M12	1983	
A865KNA	Ford Transit 190	Dixon Lomas	M12	1983	
JHF824	Volvo B10M-61	Duple Laser	C51F	1984	
JHF825	Volvo B10M-61	Duple Laser	C51F	1984	Ex Parks, Hamilton, 1986
716GRM	Volvo B10M-61	Duple Laser	C51F	1984	
184XNO	Volvo B10M-61	Duple Laser	C51F	1984	Ex Globe, Barnsley, 1986
629LFM	Volvo B10M-61	Van Hool Alizée	C53F	1985	Ex Shearings, 1991
E701WNE	Mercedes-Benz 507D	Made-to-Measure	C16F	1988	
E702WNE	Mercedes-Benz 507D	Made-to-Measure	C16F	1988	
F433ENB	Mercedes-Benz 609D	Made-to-Measure	C21F	1988	
848AFM	Volvo B10M-61	Van Hool Alizée	C53F	1989	
H490BND	Mercedes-Benz 609D	Made-to-Measure	C24F	1990	Ex Roger Hill, Congleton, 1991

Previous Registrations:

152ENM	EYK513V	848AFM	F338SMD	JHF825	A731HFP
184XNO	B359DWF	ACA194A	BKD557X	JHF826	KWJ864W
296HFM	RFM386V	ACA507A	UNO823W	PMB287Y	LDM72Y, 848AFM
505BRM	XAO3Y	ASV237	JSJ431W	PMB294Y	LDM73Y, 629LFM
629LFM	B313UNB	HOI7544	JJU440V	UTF119	NGD941V
716GRM	B637LJU	JHF824	B636LJU		

Livery: White, mauve and yellow

Walkers Executive operate this Volvo B10M with Duple Laser bodywork and now carrying a
registration 505BRM. It was photographed in Chester Bus Station in September 1993.
Richard Eversden

WARRINGTON

Warrington Borough Transport Ltd, Wilderspool Causeway, Warrington,
Cheshire, WA4 6PT

1	F101XEM	Dennis Dominator DDA1017	East Lancashire	H51/37F	1988		
2	F102XEM	Dennis Dominator DDA1017	East Lancashire	H51/37F	1988		
3	F103XEM	Dennis Dominator DDA1017	East Lancashire	H51/37F	1988		
4	F104XEM	Dennis Dominator DDA1017	East Lancashire	H51/37F	1988		

5-16   Leyland Atlantean AN68A/1R   East Lancashire   H45/31F   1978-80

5	XTB5T	8	XTB8T	11	XTB11T	13	GEK13V	15	GEK15V
6	XTB6T	9	XTB9T	12	GEK12V	14	GEK14V	16	GEK16V
7	XTB7T	10	XTB10T						

17-22   Leyland Atlantean AN68B/1R   East Lancashire   H45/31F   1980-81

17	HED17V	19	MEK19W	20	MEK20W	21	MEK21W	22	MEK22W
18	MEK18W								

23	MEK23W	Leyland Atlantean AN68C/1R	East Lancashire	H45/31F	1981		

24-28   Leyland Atlantean AN68C/1R   East Lancashire   H45/33F   1981

24	OTB24W	25	OTB25W	26	OTB26W	27	OTB27W	28	OTB28W

37	A207DTO	Leyland Olympian ONLXB/1R	East Lancashire	H45/31F	1984	Ex Derby, 1987
38	A206DTO	Leyland Olympian ONLXB/1R	East Lancashire	H45/31F	1984	Ex Derby, 1987
39	A209DTO	Leyland Olympian ONLXB/1R	East Lancashire	H45/31F	1984	Ex Derby, 1987
40	A210DTO	Leyland Olympian ONLXB/1R	East Lancashire	H45/31F	1984	Ex Derby, 1987

41-48   Dennis Dominator DDA156   East Lancashire   H51/37F*   1982/83   *43-46 are type DDA159

41	CLV41X	43	CLV43X	46	A746GFY	47	A747GFY	48	A748GFY
42	CLV42X	45	A745GFY						

51-60   Daimler Fleetline CRG6LXB   Northern Counties   H43/32F   1973-76   Ex Greater Manchester, 1987/88

51	PRJ498R	53	LJA473P	55	LJA484P	56w	LJA475P	60	YNA307M
52	LJA472P	54	LJA480P						

67	YNA295M	Daimler Fleetline CRG6LXB	Northern Counties	H43/32F	1973	Ex GM Buses, 1988
68	YNA316M	Daimler Fleetline CRG6LXB	Northern Counties	H43/32F	1974	Ex GM Buses, 1988
70	LED70P	Bristol RESL6G	East Lancashire	B41F	1976	
71	LED71P	Bristol RESL6G	East Lancashire	B44F	1976	
72	LED72P	Bristol RESL6G	East Lancashire	DP40F	1976	
73	LED73P	Bristol RESL6G	East Lancashire	B44F	1976	

74-83   Leyland Atlantean AN68A/1R   East Lancashire   H45/31F*   1977/78   *77 is H45/33F

74	TTB74S	76	TTB76S	78	TTB78S	80	TTB80S	82	TTB82S
75	REK75R	77	REK77R	79	TTB79S	81	TTB81S	83	TTB83S

Upper Left: **This Volvo B10M-61/Van Hool coach was new in 1984 to Smith Shearings of Wigan. It was acquired by Warrington for its Coach Lines unit in 1989, and was numbered C2, CIW7633. It is normally employed on private hire work.**

Lower left: **MidiLines is a marketing name for Warrington's midibus operation. This section of the fleet has 13 Carlyle-bodied Dennis Darts out of a total of 35. No.215, H843NOC, was new in 1991 and is a 35-seat vehicle. Carlyle coachworks frequently registered their products in Birmingham prior to delivery, hence the registration.**

Although painted in the pale blue, dark blue and yellow livery of Warrington's Coachlines unit, this East Lancashire-bodied Dennis Dominator is working the Warrington-Leigh local service 419. The vehicle is one of six double deck coaches in the fleet.

Opposite: The latest vehicles to enter the Warrington fleet are a further batch of Northern Counties-bodied Dennis Darts, again in the modern blue and yellow scheme. Illustrating the type is 221, K221VTB, photographed in Warrington centre. *Malc McDonald*

Warrington operate six Dodge S56 minibus with Northern Counties bodywork in the MiniLines fleet. No.205, D105TTJ, is the penultimate vehicle in the batch and is seen awaiting departure from Warrington for Penketh.

84	CLV84X	Leyland Olympian ONLXB/2R	East Lancashire	H51/37F	1982
85	CLV85X	Leyland Olympian ONLXB/2R	East Lancashire	H51/37F	1982
86	A486HKB	Leyland Olympian ONLXB/2R	East Lancashire	H51/37F	1984
87	A487HKB	Leyland Olympian ONLXB/2R	East Lancashire	H51/37F	1984
91	B101SED	Leyland Olympian ONLXCT/2R	East Lancashire	DPH47/31F	1985
92	B102SED	Leyland Olympian ONLXCT/2R	East Lancashire	DPH47/31F	1985

95-99

	Dennis Dominator DDA1017	East Lancashire	H51/37F	1989

95	F95STB	96	F96STB	97	F97STB	98	F98STB	99	F99STB

100	C100UBC	Dennis Dominator DDA1010	East Lancashire	H46/33F	1986	Ex Leicester, 1989
101	C101UBC	Dennis Dominator DDA1010	East Lancashire	H46/33F	1986	Ex Leicester, 1989
102	C102UBC	Dennis Dominator DDA1010	East Lancashire	H46/33F	1986	Ex Leicester, 1989
103	C103UBC	Dennis Dominator DDA1010	East Lancashire	H46/33F	1986	Ex Leicester, 1909
107	GHC519N	Leyland Atlantean AN68/1R	East Lancashire	H43/32F	19/5	Ex Eastbourne, 1988
108	GHC522N	Leyland Atlantean AN68/1R	East Lancashire	H43/32F	1975	Ex Eastbourne, 1988
109	GHC524N	Leyland Atlantean AN68/1R	East Lancashire	H43/32F	1975	Ex Eastbourne, 1988
110	GHC525N	Leyland Atlantean AN68/1R	East Lancashire	H43/32F	1975	Ex Eastbourne, 1988
111	UFV113R	Leyland Atlantean AN68A/2R	East Lancashire	H50/36F	1976	Ex Preston, 1990
112	UFV116R	Leyland Atlantean AN68A/2R	East Lancashire	H50/36F	1976	Ex Preston, 1990
113	UFV117R	Leyland Atlantean AN68A/2R	East Lancashire	H50/36F	1976	Ex Preston, 1990
114	UFV120R	Leyland Atlantean AN68A/2R	East Lancashire	H50/36F	1976	Ex Preston, 1990
121	F121XEM	Dennis Dominator DDA1018	East Lancashire	DPH47/29F	1988	
122	F122XEM	Dennis Dominator DDA1018	East Lancashire	DPH47/29F	1988	
148	BED729C	Leyland PD2/40 Sp	East Lancashire	H34/30F	1965	

201-206

	Renault-Dodge S56	Northern Counties	B22F	1987	201 is DP20F

201	D101TTJ	203	D103TTJ	204	D104TTJ	205	D105TTJ	206	D106TTJ
202	D102TTJ								

207-219

	Dennis Dart 9SDL3003	Carlyle Dartline	B35F*	1991	*212 is DP32F

207	H879LOX	210	H887LOX	213	H841NOC	216	H844NOC	218	H846NOC
208	H881LOX	211	H889LOX	214	H842NOC	217	H845NOC	219	H847NOC
209	H886LOX	212	H897LOX	215	H843NOC				

220	J10WBT	Dennis Dart 9SDL3003	Northern Counties Paladin	B33F	1991

221-225

	Dennis Dart 9SDL3003	Northern Counties Paladin	B33F	1993

221	K221VTB	222	K222VTB	223	K223VTB	224	K224VTB	225	K225VTB

226-235

	Dennis Dart 9SDL3034	Northern Counties Paladin	B33F	1994

226	L226SWM	228	L228SWM	230	L230SWM	232	L232SWM	234	L234SWM
227	L227SWM	229	L229SWM	231	L231SWM	233	L233SWM	235	L235SWM

C1	G100TDJ	Volvo B10M-61	Van Hool Alizée	C49FT	1989	
C2	CIW7633	Volvo B10M-61	Van Hool Alizée	C49FT	1984	Ex Shearings, 1989
C3	E256MMM	Van Hool T815H	Van Hool Alicron	C49FT	1992	Ex Dunn-Line, Nottingham, 1993
C4	D614MVR	Volvo B10M-61	Van Hool Alizée	C53F	1987	Ex Shearings, 1993
C5	WBT851	Volvo B10M-61	Van Hool Alizée	C49FT	1984	Ex Park's, Hamilton, 1989
C6	H6CLW	Van Hool T815H	Van Hool Alicron	C49FT	1991	
C7	H7CLW	Van Hool T815H	Van Hool Alicron	C49FT	1991	
C8	C108AFX	Volvo B10M-61	Plaxton Paramount 3500 III	C49FT	1986	Ex Holmes, Cheshunt, 1990
C9	G758ELV	Volvo B10M-60	Van Hool Alizée	C49FT	1990	
C10	465FBC	Aüwaerter Neoplan N122/3	Aüwaerter Skyliner	CH55/16CT	1984	Ex Stockdale, Selby, 1990
C11	611LFM	Aüwaerter Neoplan N122/3	Aüwaerter Skyliner	CH55/16CT	1984	Ex Glenfield, London SW17, 1990
C12	E777VDA	Volvo B10MD-53	Plaxton Paramount 4000	CH55/12CT	1988	Ex Flight's, Birmingham, 1991
C14	J414AWF	Volvo B10M-60	Van Hool Alizée	C53F	1992	
C15	J410AWF	Volvo B10M-60	Van Hool Alizée	C53F	1992	

Previous Registrations:

CIW7633	A185MNE	WBT851	A603UGD
CIW708	A767HPF	465FBC	A105MWT
NOI1425	EYH803V	611LFM	A334UFE, 5142SC, A384XGG

Livery: Red and white; Coaches and Dennis Darts are blue and yellow.

Still undertaking stage duties are four Bristol RESLs with East Lancashire bodywork. Seen in Knutsford on the infrequent weekday service to Lower Peover is 73, LED73P. *Graham Ashworth*

The bus station is Warrington is a hive of activity and East Lancashire-bodied Dennis Dominator 97, F97STB, is seen arriving during the early evening having worked a contract. The extensive use of East Lancashire coachwork, especially with the deeper windscreens, is a feature of Warrington's double deck fleet . *Bill Potter*

WARRINGTONS

WN & SM Warrington, The Cottage, Ilam,Ashbourne, Derbyshire, DE6 2AZ

SFP829X	Bedford SB5	Duple Dominant	C41F	1981
A529DNR	Mercedes-Benz L307D	Reeve Burgess	M12	1983
B898DCA	Mercedes-Benz L608D	PMT Hanbridge	B21F	1985
E905EAY	Bedford YMP	Plaxton Paramount 3200 III	C43F	1987
H153DJU	Dennis Javelin 11SDL1921	Plaxton Paramount 3200 III	C53F	1990
J733KBC	Dennis Javelin 11SDL1921	Plaxton Paramount 3200 III	C53F	1991
K2KHW	Leyland DAF 400	Autobus Classique	M16	1992
L545MRA	Ford Transit VE6	Ford/TCH	M14	1993

Previous Registrations:
K2KHW   K959EWF

Livery: Red and cream

Warringtons of Ilam have run services from the Dovedale area to Ashbourne and Leek for many years. SFP829X has been a faithful provider of these runs from new and provides the now-rare chance to sample a Bedford SB on service. It is seen after leaving its home village, heading for Thorpe.
Graham Ashworth

WILLIAMSONS

H J Williamson, 118 Longden Coleham, Shrewsbury, Shropshire, SY3 7HG

Depot: Knockin Heath; Shrewsbury.

RGS93R	Leyland Leopard PSU3E/4R	Plaxton Supreme III	C53F	1977	Ex Hellyers Coaches, Fareham, 1989
TPJ282S	Bedford YLQ	Plaxton Supreme III	C45F	1978	Ex Parry, Ruyton XI Towns, 1993
GWC31T	Leyland Leopard PSU3E/4R	Plaxton Supreme IV	C53F	1979	Ex Frost, Leigh-on-Sea, 1988
BAW1T	Leyland Leopard PSU3E/4R	Duple Dominant	B63F	1979	Ex Elcock Reisen, Madeley, 1984
DTY352W	Volvo B58-61	Plaxton Supreme IV	C57F	1981	Ex Owen, Oswestry, 1987
UBW788	Leyland PSU5C/4R	Plaxton Supreme IV	C53F	1981	Ex Hown, Barnoldswick, 1993
C167VRE	Ford Transit 190	PMT	B16F	1986	Ex PMT, 1987
D532HNW	Ford Transit 190	Carlyle	B16F	1987	Ex Star Line, Knutsford, 1989
F44CTX	Leyland Tiger TRCTL11/3ARZM	Duple 320	C61F	1989	Ex Bebb, Llantwit Fardre, 1991
F59YBO	Leyland Tiger TRCTL11/3ARZM	Duple 320	C61F	1989	Ex Bebb, Llantwit Fardre, 1991
G381JBD	LAG	LAG Panoramic	C49FT	1989	
H761RNT	Van Hool T815H	Van Hool Alizée	C49FT	1991	
J327VAW	Dennis Dart 9.8SDL3004	Carlyle Dartline	B40F	1991	
J328VAW	Dennis Dart 9.8SDL3004	Carlyle Dartline	B40F	1991	
K870ANT	Volvo B10M-60	Jonckheere Deauville P599	C53FT	1992	
K871ANT	Dennis Dart 9.8SDL3012	Marshall SPV C37	B43F	1992	
K152DNT	EOS E180Z	EOS 200	C53FT	1993	
K153DNT	EOS E180Z	EOS 200	C52FT	1993	

Previous Registrations:
UBW788   SLJ388X

Livery: Green and yellow
Shrewsbury Park & Ride: J327/8VAW, K871ANT.

Williamsons Motorways has been established in Shrewsbury for 75 years. It is very appropriate that they have operated the daily Park and Ride service from the Harlescott car park to the town centre since its inception. The vehicles used are the three Dennis Darts. J328VAW, shown here outside the Midland Bank, is one of the original pair bodied by Carlyle. A special livery is used for these vehicles and the reserve, BAW1T.
Bill Potter

WORTHEN TRAVEL

D A Pye, Main Road, Worthen, Shrewsbury, Shropshire, SY5 9HW

KTX244L	Bristol RESL6G	Eastern Coach Works	B47F	1973	Ex Tanat Valley, Pentrefelin, 1993
HRR759N	Bedford YRT	Plaxton Elite III Express	C53F	1975	Ex Gela, Knockin, 1989
JEA884N	Leyland Leopard PSU5/4R	Plaxton Elite III	C57F	1975	Ex Clews, Sutton, 1993
URN216R	Leyland LeopardPSU5A/4R	Duple Dominant	C51F	1976	Ex Brookfield, Stockport, 1992
SDD145R	Leyland Leopard PSU3E/4R	Plaxton Supreme III	C53F	1977	Ex Birmingham Coach Co, Smethwick, 1989
FIL6676	DAF MB200DKTL600	Plaxton Supreme IV	C57F	1981	Ex Sattelite Coaches, Worcester, 1992
FO8933	DAF SB2305DHS585	Plaxton Paramount 3200	C57F	1983	Ex Morris Travel, Pencoed, 1991
AJF88A	Bova FHD12.280	Bova Futura	C49FT	1984	Ex Silver Coach Lines, Edinburgh, 1989

Previous Registrations:

AJF88A	From new		FIL6676	PRM971X	F08933	THB430Y

Livery: Two-tone Green

There has been a coach operator based at Worthen - midway between Shrewsbury and Montgomery since the 1920s. The present operator is Worthen Travel and they operate the service linking these two towns. Seen on layover on the new Shrewsbury bus station is HRR759N, a Bedford YRT with Plaxton Elite Express III bodywork. Note the different markings from the Elite to the Supreme III. This vehicle was new to Barton Transport. *Phillip Stephenson*

ISBN 1 897990 04 9
Published by *British Bus Publishing*
The Vyne, 16 St Margarets Drive, Wellington,
Telford, Shropshire, TF1 3PH

Printed by Graphics & Print
Unit A13, Stafford Park 15
Telford, Shropshire, TF3 3BB